CONVEYOR OF THE SAYER

Conveyor of the Sayer

Billy Shaw

To order additional copies of this book, contact:
Xlibris Corporation
1-888-795-4274
www.Xlibris.com
Orders@Xlibris.com
124881

Contents

In Appreciation

I would like to thank the following individuals for inspiring me to write these poems:

Madame H. P. Blavatsky   Shaka Zulu
Rudolf Steiner   Mahatma Gandhi
Harold W. Percival   Dr. Martin Luther King Jr.
Andrew Jackson Davis   John Fitzgerald Kennedy
Jane Roberts   Malcolm X
Edgar Cayce   Bruce Lee
Carlos Castaneda   W. E. Du Bois
Haile Selassie   Kahlil Gibran

And all who have come before me to pave the way for so many,
in order that we may all walk
with dignity, honor, integrity, self-respect,
and with respect for others.

Thank You

I would like to give an honorable mention and *thanks* to those whom without their help, this book would not have been made. Mike Aguilar, John Frazier, Julie Valencia, and my best friend Michelle Autry whose dedication and insight made this book complete!

I *thank* you all! *I love you all.*

Sincerely,
Billy Shaw

I dedicate this book of poetry
to my *one* and only child—
my lovely and sweet daughter
Nyechelle Shaw.

Love,
Daddy

My Heroes

I'd like to dedicate these lines to those whom I revere

Here's to Madame Helena Petrovna Blavatsky,
Whose pioneering spirit brought the truth to light.
In her search for knowledge, she traveled very far.
She paved the way for many like a bright and shining
star.

Cheers to Shaka Zulu,
Whose spirit still rules his land.
He was a king of kings, destined from birth to be a
mighty man. His courage was his foundation, and
wisdom was his guide.
His legacy remains with his people, who live and die
with pride.

Here's to Mahatma Gandhi,
A spirit true as gold,
Whose life was written in destiny long before it was
told.
Meekness was his character; being humble he knew no
shame,
If ever there were a man of God, Gandhi was the same.

Cheers to Dr. Martin Luther King Jr.,
Whose compassion for the oppressed stirred his spirit
from within,
Chose to confront the oppressor—again and again and
again!
His faith was inspired by vision, hopes, and dreams,
Whose ideas are rooted in my heart and has
strengthened my self-esteem.

Cheers to John Fitzgerald Kennedy,
A man born to lead.
He took a stand for every man and began to plant a
seed.
In his prime, he spoke of hope, but time was not on his
side.
His memory is a memorial to all who know how he
lived and died.

Here's to Malcolm X,
A trailblazer chosen among a few.
He spoke at first against the people most commonly
known as Jews.
He resisted at first, but truth prevailed,
And his mind was turned from hate.
The truth he found along the path, but lies had sealed
his fate.
In each and every one of us, there's a Malcolm in you
and me, regardless of your opinion, he died to set us
free.

Cheers to Bruce Lee,
Whose fame framed his name.
His brilliant talent in the martial arts put other arts to
shame.
Young and bold, he taught the truth to many
privileged few.
He entertained us with his style and his popularity
grew.
At his peak, he was the best,
Accepting nothing less.
He lived his life, achieved his fame, and now he's laid
to rest.

These are the people who inspired me the most.
Here's a glass, I lift it high and give them all a toast.
Cheers to their courage that made them able and
strong.
Cheers to their dedication, may their memories live on
and on.
Here's a toast to their spirit, which compelled them all
to speak.
Here's a toast to their lives, they lived it so unique.

They inspired the young, the middle-aged, and the old.
They lived the lives of legends that build the timeless
roads.
They spoke of truth and love and fought for equality.
They died enduring injustice for people like you and
me.

They encouraged everyone and all to love one another,
Regardless of your color,
You're my sister, you
You're my brother.

Harmony was their undertaking, utopia they sought.
Peace was their purpose that no money could have
bought.
Compassion ruled their hearts, to help the oppressed.
They gave their all too many, and many for it were
blessed.
Gratitude came plenty, much love they received.
They gave hope to the hopeless, and unbelievers
believed.

Great were their examples, as history can attest.
Being greatly admired, their stories are our pretexts.
Cheers to their victory, to truth they paved the way
So that all that would could follow to Victory's
glorious day.

These are my heroes, who dedicated their lives
To uplifting the spirit of justice, which had been so
undeniably deprived.
Here's to their memory that lives on in us all.
Cheers to their vision of the future; may we equally
heed the call.

5/14/96

A Message to the Black Man

Let those in authority over you
believe that they do. But always know, black man, that you
have no
masters—in this world or in any other—as long as you know
who
you are and where you come from. And when you know this
truth,
you will never be a slave. And the truth will set you free from
ever
believing or being a slave, even when you have those in
authority
who oppose you because of their ignorance and fear. Always
know
and remember your place as a black man. You represent the
image
of God in the fullness of your blackness. You represent the
pride of
your heritage because your ancestors, who once ruled the
earth,
endowed through genetic ingenuity and intelligence your DNA
with
divine wisdom. And as divine co-creators with the Creator,
you
have within you the primary code of life—to establish
yourselves
as the true sons of God, and as such, you are the true leaders
in
the world of men. As watchers and sentinels, your legacy is to

fulfill prophecy by being fruitful and multiplying and replenishing
and subduing the world—by any means necessary. Fear not, black
man, now is the time to take your place as the true leaders of this
world and beyond. Black man, it is your destiny to fulfill the
prophecies and to speak to your people and remind them that it's
time to wake up and take a stand as the true leaders of this world
and beyond. For God so deems it. So let it be written, so let it be
said, so let it be done. *Ashanti-ki-tue.*

A Message to the Black Woman

To all the black Nubian queens, hold your head up high and be proud of your beautiful dark skin and bow down to no masters. For you are the idea created in the image of the mother goddess in earth form. Created from the dark core, beneath the crust of the earth, you are the dark matter that contains the seed of life, for within you is the secret alchemy of life in creation that transforms dark matter into imperial brilliant light. The light, which is the seed and essence of all beginnings, new and old, far and near, for your mystery and secrets, reveal your revelation to all who desire to know and dwell in the deep wells of your being. To see you is to behold the goddess within, in all its beautiful magnified glory—personified and animated by divine grace when you move and speak. There is no mineral or element in or beneath the earth nor anything created by man nor anything in the universe and beyond that personifies and magnifies beauty more than you, my black Nubian queen. You are a precious jewel that few can find, for your worth is priceless. Your eyes are the diamonds that reveal your deep, inner soul, which speaks of unfathomable love, and your smile shines like the sun that reveals the light in your heart, and your heart holds the mystery and hidden wisdom of love and its passion for life. Your knowledge and wisdom and nurturing spirit consoles the childlike and sometimes immature nature of men.

Few men ever prove or ever achieve your level or standard of worthiness because there are few men who really appreciate your position as a black Nubian queen because they rarely appreciate and understand and love themselves nor do they know their place as yet. And so to my beautiful black Nubian queens, although you seem to be all alone in your silent despair, remember this, you are not alone. And as you wait in silent prayer, as all of nature does, in high expectancy for the sons of God. The real black man is arising like the sun in the east, ready to take his place as the true leaders of the world and beyond, and then my black Nubian queen you will take your rightful place next to your black king and rule the world with divine mind and pride with honor, knowledge, and wisdom, side by side. And as the true mothers of this world and beyond, you will teach mankind with grace and knowledge and wisdom and power—the divine truth about existence here in this world and beyond. Be patient, my beautiful black queens, the sons of God are slowly awakening even today; it is the appointed time, and soon you will be glad and your years of despair will be no more. The day of reckoning has come, and the chosen ones—the black man and his beautiful black Nubian queen as gods and goddesses—will take their rightful place. And their power and glory and legacy will reign forever.

My Declaration

I pronounce today and from here on that I—in the knowledge of the spirit of the highest truth, love, liberty, and justice—do solemnly swear to uphold and represent the highest principle invested in me to wage an eternal war against racial intolerance, oppression, ignorance, police brutality, and perversion of any and all forms, morally and legally.

I now vow an oath with militancy to take a stand for the oppressed, the poor, the underdog who fights a ceaseless war for the unwanted, the neglected, the downtrodden part of humanity, whose voices are unheard because of the oppressors' vices and twisted laws that bind and bounds their minds and spirit with lies, threats, and violence and even death for exposing their evil ways.

I also speak for those who are falsely imprisoned for standing up and beholding their principles, sacrificing family, freedom, acceptance, and sometimes risking their own lives for the sake of justice and truth.

I now petition to the higher powers that be, to strengthen me with the will and the power and the wisdom and the courage to confront the enemy, whenever and whomever they might be, and prepare in defiance to assault the enemy with the weapons of truth and justice and to seek and destroy with a vengeance all their illogical, false sense of security and superiority with the knowledge of profound morality and divine truth. God compels me.

01/08/05

My Creed

The prime directive is self-preservation
at all cost, by any means necessary.
That means to not let anybody disrespect
you, demean you in any way, form, or fashion.
Always stand up for your principles and rights.
And remember, you do make a difference.

03/03/03

I Speak

I speak of revolution
The motion that moves
Through time
I speak of revelation
That inspires the
Heart and mind
I speak of tribulations
The trials for all mankind
I speak of a solution
And now is the time
I speak of a proposition
Opposed by popular view
I speak of a change in direction
A choice taken by the few
I speak of preparation
That may prepare us now
I speak from the spirit
I will show you how.

8-17-97

The Voice

I speak from within, hear me now
I'll tell you which way and show you how
I have spoken but you have not heard
You inclined your ear but did not hear a word
Listen quietly and take heed
I give the water and plant the seed
The moment has come so make your choice
I am the word, now hear my voice
The time has come, behold the call
This message comes from within to everyone and all
What you've been seeking and hoping to find
Is not found in books but in the heart and mind
So listen closely as I reveal
This message is of the spirit, and to yours I appeal
From the heights of the heavens
And down into the bellows of the deep
Long before creation when minds did sleep
We were one in union together
And we will be one in the future forever
So this is the message, and this is true
At that day you shall know, that I am in my
Father, and you in me, and I in you. John 14:20

8/5/1997

Destiny

There is an intruder in my life. It knows all my weaknesses
But it also underestimates my strength
It breaches all bearers, trying to kill my resolve to live
It ultimately desires my death. But again it does not
understand
Nor does it know the depth of my will
I am born a conqueror
A warrior with a zeal and a shield of passion
I know my enemy well, its tactics and methods
To divert me from my cause is vanity to the extreme
Its dangerous vices surround me with every intent
To pry me with all vanities and temptations. But I, with all
intent
I endure and prevail against the known foe. I fight on
With every ounce and fiber of my being; there is no other way
I am courage abound; my journey is fret with adversity and
obstacles that would thwart my success; I know who I am
And I say to the enemy with all the compelling spirit of God
I rebuke you, spirit of confusion, you spirit of doubt
You adversary. You liar. Deceiver.
You who brood in the mind of subconsciousness and
Idleness.

I live on! It is my destiny!
12/08/2005

Revelation

If you would like to know me, I'll explain what I can. I've been called
eccentric, complex at the most, complicated and incomprehensible, deep and
intelligent, intellectual, spiritual, and strange. I've also been called crazy,
psycho, mad, loony, possessed, etc.

But besides all the misunderstanding and misinterpretations and adulations
and compliments, I am just a man.
The impelling mysteries that we seek to understand are not far from us. The
unknown mysteries are within us to find. You are centered and connected to
the source, referred as the essence.
You are one with everything, its cause and effect and presence. Its eminence
is manifested in its image of which you temporarily embody.
You are its majestic embodiment, behold.
If you thought and saw and you believed and received I and all, and all and
I inspired what you conceived.

For we are one, eternally bound, our realities are intimately
mixed.
Although interchangeably tangible, your ways, our thoughts
are linked
To beingness beyond mere words' description, to depths and
heights that
defy comprehension.
Our worlds of light that accedes to heights of magnificent,
awesome
ascension.

Here the light of consciousness has its true domain. We're all
emerged in
Lightness, in a dimension all for you to attain.
Be not dismayed by what you have yet to know, for it is your
evolution and
destiny; your future has been foretold.

12/14/05

Paradox

I've seen the unseen with invisible
Eyes
I know the unknowable without
Reason of mind
I heard the inaudible
Without any ears
I spoke the unspeakable without
Use of words
I thought the unimaginable
Without conception
I've been were there is no place or
Time
And I've come to the conclusion
That there are no guarantees,
Or absolute reasoning for just
One cause
Truth is a paradox explaining
Nothing

4-23-09

My Truth

I write you this letter to tell you the truth
How it is, how it was, from now since my youth
I've struggled and strived and did my best
I did what I could, and God did the rest
I've endured pain and sorrow
I suffered in silence of not knowing what will be tomorrow
I've been alone and lived with doubt
I've been down in despair, but don't count me out
I've endured the pounding of the blacksmith's steel
The grain has been shifted, locked, and sealed
Like a phoenix I arise from the ashes and fly through the air
Over the mountains and above the clouds—wherever I might
dare
Singing about today and praising tomorrow
Thinking about the future and letting the past go with all its
despair and sorrow
I arise standing tall, ready for the day
Seeking new challenges, come what may
Having new hopes and a brand-new vision
Choosing to do better and making better decisions
I am a man, and this is my truth
This is how it is, from now since my youth.

02-22-96

Blessed Bliss

Standing on the edge of time on the
Horizon of imagination, I saw the
Unimaginable, I witness the ocean of it
All, it spanned the space of eternity, its
Power was awesome, I was petrified
With fear, I don't know why, and at the
Same time, I was in awe of its
Magnificence, captivated by the
Specter of its eminence, I could only
Look upon it for so long as the fear
Took over my sense, and I stepped back
And slowly turned away from the sight
Before me, as I felt its powerful force
Pulling me, drawing me into its deep
Waters, I saw a church away off, and I
Walked toward it, and I entered it, and I
Found solace and sanctuary in the
Church, but I have no doubt that what I
Had just witness would find me again
Someday, and the next time, I will be
Willing, and I will submerge myself in
Blessed bliss for eternity.

2-13-09

The Presence

Seeing I saw a presence not to far from
me
Its being was permeating an essence
Something inside of me
Was led by a light, guiding me to see
Something of another something just
Like me
A familiar thought exposed me to a
Distant memory
Of what I know before, of what I
Yearned to see
A vision of an image, an idea of what
Will be
My mind's eye behold me seeing that I see
Receptive to the presence of what I
Know is me
I know beyond an answer, I am more than
What I see

2-11-09

Mystory

I'm dying inside, but God won't let me
So much pressure, I feel so empty
Which way should I turn, where do I go
I ain't got no money, ain't got nothing to show
My past behind me, but it haunts my mind
I think about movin', but my future is blind
Too much trouble, so what's the use
Can't get past the memory of mental abuse
I was raised in this life of mental insanity
After forty-six years, I still ain't free
Got a family to raise and bills to pay
I take pills to live from day to day
Death and taxes, and troubles rule the world
Gotta find a way to support my baby girl
I'm caught up in debt, but behind the times
I need some release to ease my mind
I hustle on the streets, grinding and grinding
I play by the rules, but I'm rewinding and finding
That the rules keep changing from time to time
Walking through life, avoiding land mines
Tossed to and fro by waves of turbulence
Trying to stand up, but can't find my balance
Somebody help me, I'm going overboard
I'm sending out an SOS, help me, Lord
I'm legally in a prison, set upon me
I got no rights, where others are free
I'm black, broke, and homeless, bound by poverty
Looking for an opportunity to set me free
I've been condemned by a crime that ain't my fault
I tried to raise myself but was convicted by default

I was born to die and live through hell
I been on my own since I was twelve
I've been rejected and neglected, and that's my story
It's still the same, add the stress and worry
It's a fucked up life, when poverty is a crime
Your folks don't help you, won't give me a dime
I'm so tired, so tired beyond belief
I need a new life, I need some relief
When will it stop, when will it cease
I need some help, I need some peace
It's sad to say, but I have to admit
I'm a victim of a crime that ain't never given me shit.

01/27/2008

Skid Row

Lost in limbo with nowhere to go
Soon to be released back to Skid Row
Lost in limbo with so much on my mind
Back to a world, trying to find
A place called home just for me
But there's no place called home for me, you see
Like a ship in the ocean with nowhere to go
Stuck in a limbo called Skid Row
It's a bad situation living downtown
The people don't smile, they just frown
Can't trust the neighbors, can't trust your friends
Can't trust your brother nor next of kin
The police are worse, they'll put you in jail
They'll set you up if you don't tell
Too much drugs, too much crime
Too much poverty, can't save a dime
What's gonna happen, where do I go
Lost in limbo back to Skid Row
Somebody help me, I'm running out of time
So much misery, I'm losing my mind
So much confusion, so much hate
Somebody save me before it's too late
I don't want to go, but what choice do I got
My life's so meaningless. Is this my lot?
I try to be patient, but what's the use
I'm drained of purpose, I need a boost
I'm tired of living with nowhere to go
God, save me from this place called Skid Row

1/18/2006

If Only You Knew

Here I sit under a tree
Free as the birds that fly over me
The sun is shining, casting its light
For now, for the moment, I feel all right
Life is in session, fleeting as the air
The love of life clears all despair
Beauty cascading, no room to despond
I am truth, I knew it all along
What else can I say? I cannot lie
You won't believe me, I know the reason why
For the truth is not in you, and that's why I sigh
Not in vain do I speak, patients make me wait
I've done it all before, so it's never too late
If only you could see and understand
If only you knew of the mysteries of man
I'd really like to teach you and show you the way
But will you listen to what I have to say?
Light is dim, and ignorance rules the night
Everyone's confused 'cause they won't do right
Hear my voice, oh fleeting dawn
I am spirit, nature sings my song
Love is no wonder, its mystery revealed
Your purpose is questioned, to truth
You must yield,
What will it take, oh complex man
Will you finally wake up when I come again?

Will you?

05-13-96

I Wonder

Here I am as I sit and ponder
Thinking about life and all its wonder
I'm besieged by mystery and various world opinions
About other realms of existence and spiritual
dimension
Life after life or life after death
Does life continue when there's no body left
Celestial terrestrial life in space
Is there more intelligence than the human race
Exoteric esoteric, what more can we receive
Does knowledge have a limit, do we evolve or
recede
I contemplate mysteries, secrets of the past
I think about the future, and will mankind last
Are we on the right path, is danger in our way
Will we survive our own destruction on that
fateful day
Is there a secret process that destines our fate
Or are we only victims of the demons we create
I wonder as I write these lines, what destiny awaits
me
I wonder if some sign will come to finally wake
me
To my purpose-driven called-upon destiny to fulfill a
Desire, a compelling compulsion to do what only
The chosen few could possibly do under any
Situation, to be extraordinary, and to do
Extraordinary deeds in the most difficult times, is
It just my imagination, or is it destiny calling,

Drawing me to a greater cause than just me, if it is
My destiny, and if I am called then I will answer,
And say yes, and I will come.

3-18-09

The Time

What I'm feeling, I'm trying to express
A new way of viewing this mind-time
test
I'm thinking slowly while my mind
rewinds
Erasing my thoughts to forget the time
I cease all movement and animation
Erasing all feelings without
anticipation
Plagued by repetition, I repeat the time
Easing slowly to erase my mind
I gradually implement new intentions
While manipulating thoughts of new
inventions
With no more thoughts and nowhere or
place
I'm conscious abound to explore new
space
Floating in seclusion, I expand my mind
And fill all space, I become the time.

12-16-09

I See through God's Eyes

I see through God's eyes things so clear
I know beyond a doubt why we are here
I do not imagine nor linger in fantasy
for I am I, what is will be
I see you all from a different view
and I know for a fact that I am you
for we are one divinely integrated
without division, no longer segregated
I see through God's eyes, and now I see
the ultimate potential in you and me
there is no lack in the all in all
listen, my friends, and heed the call
beyond the past, present, and future and time
is absolute reality beyond limited mind
beyond the universes is absolute light
is glory incomprehensible beyond visible sight
I see through God's eyes things to be
I know beyond a doubt, listen to me
that all is one in conscious glory
the I is the ideal, and this is my story
with your knowledge, let wisdom incline
and believe with understanding
and then you will find
that what I say and my message to you
that all is one and all is true.

Greater than Me

Now I write my thoughts of me
I think I'd like to see within me

I'd like to have all I like
I'd like to have inner sight
I'd like to see how things could be
I'd like to know of other realities
I'd like to see in other dimensions

I'd like to know knowledge with new comprehension
I like to indulge my imagination
I like to live without fabrication
I'd like to live without limitation
I like the world without civilization

I like to dream without the time
I'd like to give you a piece of my mind
So I write with no conclusion
Immersed in thought with one inclusion

I have an idea, a vision of what I see
The vision I allude to is greater than me.

12/17/2005

Infusion

I believe in I am, and I know more, there is
More to me than I see,
I can see me from a point, but my origin is
More than I see
I am that formless being, light in
Omnipresence, ascension beyond mere
heights
Timelessness beyond comprehension
I dwell among the aeons without realm or
Dimensions merged with primal light
Essence in consciousness
I am the wind of the spirit that moves the
water
I am the blood running through the veins of
the earth
And the blood that flows through all life
animate
I am that that draws all life to it
For I am supreme desire
The complete omnipresence, omniscience
omnibeing

5-30-09

Still Waters Run Deep

Within my mind, I fathom deep beneath the
surface, beyond past sleep. I submerge
myself in objective state where my being is in
a tranquil wake, conscious, unmoved by
conscious time. Here I am immersed in mind
without a memory of conscious time. I find
myself from deep within diluting illusions
like the wind as peace and serenity unfold, (I
behold me) in the light of truth, and (I
become and see) the truth of life and love in
me. Still waters run deep, so I've been told
now I know for this truth is old. I now look
from within with a view from the past, and
I've found a revelation to all those who ask
before mystery, beyond memory, in objective
wake when absolute mind was in a perfect
state that all is one, connected together, and
we are one in the future forever.

12/22/07

Still Waters

Deep within the flesh and bones is a place of solitude called the quiet zone—where serenity and tranquility is a placid lake, where dreams are pondered upon our wake. Far beneath the skin within is mind without thought. No beginning or end: here is the peaceful objective state where mind never sleeps, always conscious and awake. Never a ripple or movement it makes, for it is the deep waters of our conscious state. Immersed in our being of pure divine love, submerged in dwellings from within and above.

10/08/07

The One

Not far from destiny is where my fate
awaits
As I travel this journey bound to
heaven's gate
I bypass history and ages of long ago
Time is transparent, invisible to the
seen
I move right through it, as if in a dream
I see points of reference, but no origin
Beyond the speed of light, reality
bends
Blending in the light, I become one
With the light of eternity, I become the
One.

5-02-09

The Son

I thought I saw a parable the writing on the wall
I read a heeded message I read a sign a call
I thought about the message and what it meant to
me
I wondered if it was inclusive or if only I could see
The writing on the wall was it meant for me
Was the message clearly telling of our fate
Or was the message saying that it was all too late
As I read on the message became so clear
It was a message of hope and explained why we are
here
It spoke of a mission taken by us all
It told of a journey and how mankind did fall
We fell from grace and lost our place
We lived in sin destroying our race
We lied and slandered one another
We fornicated in sin with our sisters and our
brothers
There was dissension and strife that caused our
division
Until one day there arose a leader who made a
decision
He spoke the words inspiring the race
Telling the people to remember their place
He reminded them all from whence they came
And called them all by their spiritual names
From that day the people became as one
Beholding the one that they now call the son

5-12-09

A Pencil's View

I am a pencil that writes with your hand
I can do nothing alone but then again
I am the instrument of communication
With my use civilizations are brought to desolation
I am the silent friend or enemy of man
My unspoken word can rebuild or destroy the land
I'd like to take the time to show you how things used to be
I'd like to take you back in a time before prehistory
On adventure through to unknown days
Back before a time when the sun shed no rays
Let's go back to when mind was a matter of space
And imagine if you can nowhere or place
Imagine mind with no conception
Unforetold nor spoken perception
Just try to concentrate on uncalculated time
And listen to the silence that envelops your mind
Realize now the reality of unconfirmed expression
Feel yourself expanding from regression to progression
Grow and glow into imperial night
Let your thought go yes give them flight
Be the wind the breeze that's everywhere
Be free and wild as the invisible air
Now if you care this is the way it used to be
And time again will know this reality
When all have evolved into the imperial night
And time again will twinkle into blissful twilight.

4-14-84

It's Time

I'll stand up for you if no one stands at all
I'll take the blame to save your name
I'll even take the fall

Your noble spirit stands alone against
The enemy's might
Inspired by your dedication I too choose
To fight

Lift up your voice and speak the truth
Till justice and liberty prevail
Let freedom ring throughout the world
While justice ring liberty bell

Stand up for something or fall for anything
The choices are yours to take
Don't make the mistake of turning the other cheek
'Cause that was our first mistake

Listen up and take heed for your very survival's
At stake
There are those you know who think you're wrong
And that's their second mistake

Look out, brotha, they're on the prowl
Their system is falling down their time is numbered
Coming to a close, it's time to stand up
And get down

1/23/2006

The Way

If I say something
That's true
And it really makes
A difference to you
Then tell all the people
You meet in your life
'Cause this is what
I intended to do

I believe in my principles and honor
I can't stand fabrication or lies
If I can dispel and squash opposition
I'd lead my people up high

Do not take your life for granted
'Cause trials and tribulations will come
And if you don't care or believe at all
Your victories will come undone

Believe in something to lift you up
When you're alone and nobody cares
Open your mind and look inside
You'll find your way from there

1/23/06

I Am Through with This World

I am through with this world, and all its temptations
I am through with this world, and its many
manifestations
I am through with this world, and perverse pornography
I am through with this world, and I am free, can't you see
I am through with this world, full of lies
I am through with this world, no more alibis
I am through with this world, with its evil intentions
I am through with this world, with its wicked inventions
I am through with this world, that's so unkind
I am through with this world, let the blind lead the
blind
I am through with this world, I want to tell my story
I am through with this world, I have found grace and
glory
I am through with this world, its trials and tribulations
I am through with this world, with its false adulations
I am through with this world, because God is love
I am through with this world, because heaven is above
I am through with this world, that bounds and binds
I am through with this world, that had my mind
I am through with this world, I was under a curse
I am through with this world, condemned at birth
I am through with this world, I made a choice
I am through with this world, now hear my voice
I am through with this world, I have been set free
I am through with this world, so let it be
I am through with this world, of confrontation

I am through with this world, of aggravation
I am through with this world, I have been changed
I am through with this world, my life has been
rearranged
I am through with this world, I have a new lease
I am through with this world, I now have peace
I am through with this world, I was blind, now I see
I am through with this world, and the world hates me
I am through with this world, it's taken its toll
I am through with this world, God has freed my soul
I am through with this world, and have a new spirit
I am through with this world, God speaks, can you hear
it
I am through with this world, my burden is light
I am through with this world, I was wrong, now I am right
I am through with this world, no more worldly
obsessions
I am through with this world, no more worldly
possessions
I am through with this world, and I am in love
I am through with this world, with my God above
I am through with this world, no worries about
tomorrow
I am through with this world, no more pain or sorrow
I am through with this world, and all its attractions
I am through with this world, no more distractions
I am through with this world, bound by liberation
I am through with this world, and its justification
I am through with this world, let the truth be told
I am through with this world, behold
I am through with this world.

2-22-09

Transition

Give me a reason, I just want to know
What is your purpose, what do you know
You said you knew something
About something I said
You provoked a debate, but your words are dead
How could you speak with no understanding?
You flounder in delusion, stupid while standing
Now listen to me and close your mouth
And let me finish what I was talking about
I'll tell you again as I told you before
There is no death, there's so much more
Life is transition, transcending all forms
Don't get caught up thinking the norm

All is transcending, impending in space
From the one-cell amoeba to the human race
There is no beginning, there is no end
Listen well and understand my friend
Evolution changes forms, and all life progresses
Revolution is inevitable that cleans man's messes
Nothing stays the same, there's nothing without change
The past seems to repeat itself because man
Remains the same
So here's your chance to change the future
As I believe and hope you do
What you need is what you got, the future
Waits for you.

1/02/06

Will

Do not misunderstand me
It's so unthoughtful and unkind
I spoke and taught the truth always
Let no doubt invade your mind

There are many misinterpretations
But the truth will always prevail
Its eternal beacon is absolution
That no symbol or translation can tell

The secrets of all mysteries
Are beyond the religions of today
Neither science nor philosophy
Can behold and direct truth's ways

From the deepest, darkest depths
The unimaginable brilliant light
There are few in number even today
Who can fathom truth's insight

What word can interpret its meaning
What image can hold its vision
With so many ways, it comes and goes
But I assure it's one without division

But seek it, my people, as you will
For its purpose for you is its delight
It triumphs in victory, compulsion's its will
Which enlightens your conscious insight.

02/02/06

The Message

I am here at last. I come from afar. A distant past I present to you from sublime time, a glimpse of the future from a memory of mine. I'll open time's corridor if you can bear to see. Look through time's window and listen to me. Here is a vision of multiple places. The course of the future depends on all races.

What you will see are potentials to be. The thoughts you think create your reality. Your survival or extinction depends on solutions. Your problems involve vain institutions. You must decide your ultimate fate and live together before it's too late.

There are contradictions that stand in your way. Religions and science must merge today.

All men must take a stand and give peace and love a helping hand.

Stop the fighting; cease the hate. Stop the conflict at Armageddon's gate.

Watch for the omens; these are the times when the past relives the future's crimes.

The choices of all are many to take. Let's not relive the past's mistakes.

The Messenger
12/17/2005

Theo-Sophia

Our unity has no bearer except in illusion
Time is relevant only if you believe it
Truth is opposed to no worthy cause
Being is limitless without comprehension
True vision is sight beyond one's eyes
Sound is refined in infinity
Light is omnipresent, omniscient, omnibeing
The incomprehensible cannot be
I is absolute
Silence is profound
Wisdom is a paradox
Knowledge is abstract

01-15-06

Karma

People say this, or people say that
But most do not care for the truth of the fact
If what is true can relieve our minds
And wisdom's secret we sought to find
Then it would behoove us to read between
And beyond the lines
For the mysteries are concealed, but there
Is no lock
But people are dulled, struck by the clock
Petrified in fear of time, which they believe
Begins and stops
Soiled in illusions, stained by lies
Their wills are fragile, afraid to try
But for those of us who seek and have
Sought
To see the truth and are willing to be
Taught
Will by honest desire come to know
That all that is, is karma—we reap what we sow.

9-21-96

Psalm from Shaw

Vanity is inevitable without sincerity;
Be patient with acquired knowledge.
Misinterpretation will prevail
If honesty is diluted by arrogance.
Death is in the soul of one who
Does not care about themselves
or others.

01-15-06

Remember Me

If any accident or mishap
should befall me,
tell them not to forget me.
If I should die before I awake,
tell them not to forget me.
If I never see the break of day,
tell them not to forget me.
If you never receive my call,
tell them not to forget me.
If you should never hear my voice,
tell them not to forget me.
If you should never see my face,
tell them not to forget me.
If they should mourn because I'm gone,
tell them never to forget me.
And when all is said and done;
remember me.

I Know

I know.

12-27-09

Virgin Virtue

virgin virtue
always right
virgin purity
clear as light
virgin innocence
diamond bright
virgin beauty
such a sight
virgin love
in the night
virgin truth
not always white

8-4-97

The Prime Directive

As cocreators with the Creator,
we are here as spiritual explorers within
creation, given the purpose and will and design to
explore creation in all its manifestations and glory.
The *prime directive* and our purpose is to imbue
the visible manifestation of life with our spiritual
consciousness so that process of the manifested
creation will continually evolve and eventually
transform into divine light. By our constant
interaction and friction with matter, we raise the
vibration of consciousness in matter until all matter
evolves and becomes individual beings of *light*
and unto itself reflecting and repeating the *osmosis*
of creation again and again into *eternity*! Life in
creation will continue to manifest itself relatively to
our *direct* and *indirect* involvement. Knowingly
and unknowingly in evolution because this is the
will of *the prime directive*,
the first cause.

9-13-11

I Am

In my thoughts
In my dreams
The sound of my mind
Is a spiritual peace
A silent breeze
Everywhere but nowhere
Its presence is I
I am at one with it
I am it
It is I
I am.

10-18-07

I Am 2

My mind's Eye is I
My I is mind
I am my mind's Eye
I and Eye is Mind
I am my mind
I am

10/13/05

Please

I am the truth, love, light, and the way
I am the moon, the stars, the sun in the day
I am comfort, tranquility, serenity, and peace
I am the first, the last, but never the least
I am the Father, the Son, and the Holy Ghost
I am grace with humility, host of hosts
I hold the universe, the earth in one hand
In the other, I hold the mysteries of man
I am the hidden, the revealed, unlike no other
I am your father, mother, sister, or brother
I now beseech you to behold these truths
And it would behoove you all to come together
And live in peace and love one another
And in the blessings of the spirit, face to face
Make a commitment to save your race
Abide in me as I abide in you
And give what you can, and do what you can do
I am coming with all my glory
You should know by now my holy story
I grant you all with surplus favor
To change your lives and modify your behavior
I love you, I do, with unconditional measure
I've granted you grace and blessings with pleasure
Life is fleeting, so please take care
There is a system called justice that's sometimes
unfair
So take the time to love one another
And give from your heart and come together,
Please.

3-07-09

The Principle

It is the ever-undeveloped primordial principle without cause or effect. It is one without division but manifested in various ways. It is the ultimate consciousness and power beyond comprehension. It is the essence of love and light. It is life in all creation. It neither expands nor retracts from any known position because there is no point of reference to its origin, because it has no beginning and no end. It is absolute without question because it is the answer of the question. Its being is present in all things without being visible because it cannot be comprehended with finite minds.

Love

I am love, and truth is my crown
the essence of light, silence profound
wisdom is light, understanding a guide
truth a pedestal, I speak it with pride
come to it, and I'll give to you
a love so sweet, a love so true
love is sweet, and I am so
I am love, I'd like you to know
love is gentle, wise, and meek
serene and peaceful, slow to speak
I am love, the heart's desire
heaven's my temple, God's empire
I am spirit, the idea of love
I am peace, my symbol's a dove
grace is my glory, radiant from within
I am your father, your mother, or a friend
I am innocence, born in its youth
I am the way, the light, and the truth
I am love, so now you've heard
I am love, and these are my words.

6/17/96

Spirit

I am will manifested and personified in creation. I am the voice in all that is spoken. I am the unknown and known. I am the mystery and the revealed. I am the darkness and the light. I am that which is beneath as well as above. I am omnipotent, omniscient, and omnibeing. I am the primordial cause of it all. I am the prime directive. I am the essence. I am the source. I am the force. I am that, I am.

Listen

I am that I am
I am the Alpha and Omega.
I am timeless without beginning.
I am the absolute, infinity without end.
I am beyond the realms of human comprehension.
I am light beyond extinction.
I am the eternal fire that permeates and exudes all life.
I am the essence that sustains the universe.
I am the primordial cause in all effects.
I am the prime directive behind all inspiration.
I am the ceaseless motion, the energy that evolves creation.
I am nothing, yet all things.
I am the Creator, the Preserver, and the Destroyer.

Words to the Wise

"In that day you will realize, that I AM in my Father.
That my Father is in me, and that I am in you."

—John 14:20

We are one, we are one, we are one.

John 10:30
Philippians 2:5
Luke 17:20

12/14/05

Behold

You do not have a clue
As to what I meant
When I told you that I'd come
For this cause I was sent
Why do you doubt or disbelieve
You do not understand
Why can't you see?
Behold, I come, and now it's time
To face the truth, to have an open mind
I am the beginning, I am the end
I am the answer, come, my friend
I am the truth you've been looking for
Behold, I knock, open the door.

8/17/97

Compassion

Be Still and know God
Be Silent and know the Truth
Be Meek and Humble
And know Peace
Be Grateful and
Be full of Grace
Be Giving and Charitable
And know the Immutable
Bountiful wealth of God's
Gift of Life

Be Patient and you shall
Perform the Will of God
In all your Getting
Get Understanding
And you will know
How to dispense
With Justice and Equality
    Compassion.

12/08/05

A Paradox

I am spirit here in eternity
Nowhere or place you can see
I am spirit, creator of many
All of it more and plenty
I am spirit, consciousness supreme
Illusion, reality, a dream
I am spirit, the prime directive
I choose not nor am I selective
I am spirit, I have no voice
I gave no directions, so make your
choice
I am spirit, no right or wrong
Good versus evil, ding or dong
I am spirit, essence or principal
The it, the all, the ever primordial
I am spirit, the fire, the light
Within, without, who is right.

2-22-09

The Message 2

How nurturing and comforting is the wisdom of the spirit. It comforts and consoles the soul of man and gives him peace, serenity, and tranquility. It leads and guides man's ways in the ways of the spirit that transcends and transports man's mind into new dimensions of consciousness, elevating man to a higher realm of being into a blissful awareness unknown to the average carnal-minded man. The evolvement of all mankind from inferior beings to superior beings is destiny; it is evolution, and revolution is a resolution to the solution in revelation. Consciousness is integrated; it is absolute. It is infantilism that cannot be comprehended by finite minds, but with instinct and intuition and imagination. We can understand it by understanding ourselves; although we are the ideal image of creation, we can never fully—without perfect understanding—comprehend the ideal. Man.

12/22/07

I Have Spoken

Surely, I have spoken in so many ways. I've spoken to you through instruments not even used today. I've spoken to you through history for generations long ago. I've spoken to you of many beginnings of one which begins today. I've given you all these opportunities to change your evil ways. I've spoken to you of trials and tribulations, the price that all must pay. What more can I offer, what more can I say. I gave up my glory and laid my life down. I put on the crown of thorns and made not a sound. I was whipped and scorned and made to feel ashamed. I picked up the cross and walked through Jerusalem. I gave my life and spirit and sacrificed for you so that all who could would follow and do as I do—through graces, gift of glory, to truth whose paths been paved so that all who choose to follow Christ's most sacred way.

10/07/07

I Hope

I paid the price for many
The cost was very high
I sacrificed my place for
You so that none of you
Should die
I gave my life for
Heaven's sake wouldn't
You have done it for me
I would like to think and
Believe you would do the
Same for me

2-05 09

It's All Karma

I see what is without any doubt
and I know without a doubt
what I'm talking about
I know without reason
and I'll try to explain
the why and the reasons
for suffering and pain
it's all about karma
cause and effect
the lame the blind
the mute and the deaf
what you do and the
choices you make
are the results of
actions and chances
you take
there are no accidents
only consequences
that is the law of justice
that karma dispenses
so with reasons as
you try to find
a reason why that
boggles the mind
that all that is
is karma
you reap what you sow.

God Speaks

I am God. How many times do I have to say it? How many ways do I have to express it? You have imagination, instinct, intuition. You have sight, hearing, smelling, touch, taste—all these functions are yours, but you still cannot see me, understand me, nor do you know me. Why are you so gullible and vulnerable, so easily misled? You have everything in the world and beyond to relate to. Why are you so disconnected? Where is your inspiration? Where is your vision? Why can't you decipher the times? Why are you so lost? I never left you, so why do you say I need to be found? Why do you wait for my return?

Such thoughts are preposterous, foolish, contradicting. There are those of you who even have the audacity to believe that I had to die on a cross to redeem mankind to myself in vindication of sin of which I am supposed to be the soul proprietor of "good God"—what a bunch of crap talk about blasphemy!

Are you people really in my image? Wake up. The time is now. I am here in the ever present. Do not look any farther, so do not worry; it's never to late. I am not far from you; in fact, as I speak, I am in your midst, and even more than that—get this—I am not only in you (here's the real punch line)—get a mirror quick—*you see, I am you.*

For references, ask a few of enlightened ones: Zarathustra, Li Po, Chin, Hiawatha, Osiris, Moses, Melchizedek, Enoch, Jesus, Buddha, Krishna, Muhammad, Maieytra, El Morya, Damador, Kahlil Gibran, Madame H. P. Blavatsky, Rudolf Steiner, Harold W. Percival, Andrew Jackson Davis, Pythagoras, Krishnamurti, Gandhi, Martin Luther King, just to name a few friends of mine. They spoke well of me.

1/15/06

A Prophecy

Here is a mystery, a secret I must tell
Not far from the future is a place called hell
Where night is a terror, and day a fright
Sunlight is rare, streetlights are bright
Gloom is common, pollution in the air
The sign of the dragon looms in despair
There is fire in the water, what is this truth
Hear the loud screams that come from the youth
Trees are petrified, hard on the ground
Due to the thunder that came without sound
Here is a clue to you who wonder
What happened here is for all to ponder
Sight upon sight shows visions of fear
See a dirty face staring, shedding a tear
Where is the hope that yesterday had fueled
Now a lifeless soul that spirit once embueled
Children of today, take heed and weep
Your father's generation has sowed, now you must reap
Here is the mystery of a tale yet told
Here is the prophecy told long of old
Here is tomorrow, the scroll is unrolled.

4-30-96

A Proverb

Here's to the future,
Behold the call
Here's to tomorrow,
May we live through it all
Hail to the *gods*,
That's you and I
Hail to the angels,
Who never lie
Hail to the one
Who dies for truth
Pray for the old men,
Who curses the youth
You who remember,
And never forget
Have love for the
Ungodly and strangers
You've never met.

3-28-96

A Christmas Carol

Thy kingdom come, thy will be done
When enlightenment illumines the way
When the heavens sing and the cymbals ring
We'll know it's Christmas day
So to all who know and to those who don't
His majesty is on his way
He brings tidings of joy that riches employ
That all may give what may.
So join me in singing and caroling, dancing
Whatever joy suits your way
'Cause Christ is coming with joy
And harmony with Christmas caroling and play.

11-02-07

Reality

For if it is the will
of conviction and not
conformity, imagine
the unimaginable
possibility of free will
for free will proves
the unequivocal
proof that the law
of karma and happenstance
is reality without boundaries
conditions and absolutes
for reality is a paradox
and can never be fully
explained by and with
finite understanding and minds.

10-07-07

Take Heed

Take heed, my friend
Of what you hear
There are sounds
So deep not meant
For ears
The symphony of
Creation is too
Much to bear
So listen, my friend
Take heed and beware
Do not trespass into
That silent night
For there are sounds
So terrible that cause
Such fright
You may be tempted
To just try one time
But believe me
When I say
You'll lose your mind
And if you do not
Heed me and try instead
You'll find your soul
Among the dead.

8-6-97

There's Nothing Higher than Truth

Check my status am I registering to you?
Am I notarized and authorized to do the do
I have authenticated legitimized my message now
I won't have no fabricated instigated words from you
So speak no litigating highlighting things you do
Why minimize autonomize my rap with you
Authenticate all my whys if you can
Prosenthesize amenimise sounds I use
Animated three dimensional worlds are cues
That virtual realities are proof for you
That artificial inorganic life exists
Even higher minded thoughts are bliss
Spirals of the conscious in the vortex
Prove once again that life beyond life exists
If you feel what I'm sayin' then hear me out
One without the other is not what it's about
Infinite celestial space or time
Soul of consciousness, spirit, and mind
1, 2, 3, or multiple places
Black, white, red, yellow, and brown races
Call your religions whatever you choose
Wherever truth is you can't lose.

11-21-07

Imitation or Life

Is death so imminent that life cannot prevail
Can we go beyond time waiting to exhale
Compelling compulsion the drive to succeed
Spirit or matter, do we evolve or recede
Is evolution a problem or solution
Do we resolve our past with vain resolutions
Stuck in time do we wish to be free
Do we take illusions as reality
When the sun shines do we turn our backs
Does wisdom flow or seeps through cracks
A gift I give, or do I take
Life is a drop, a pond, or lake
Halfway through the journey the answers will come
Moments of pleasure arise and then some
Who will be first and who will be last
Images are forming, the mold has been cast
Darkness dawns, raising the past
Time is patient, nothing ever lasts
Will I be or will I not
What does it matter time never stops.

5-1-96

Heaven

Life and light and its magnificent brilliance
Love and compassion and eternal resilience
Glory with grace and with dazzling rapture
Warmth without heat ascending the next chapter
Happiness and gratitude and laughter and play
Immersed in the light that leads the way
Through the gates to behold his throne
Drawn by this spirit from which the light shone
In a place called heaven where you'll present your case
And boldly speak to him face to face
With wisdom and love he'll tell you, you've passed
No more worries, you made it at last

2/02/06

Hell

There is no darkness, there is no light
Nothing exists no left no right
No feeling or emotions to compound
Your fear
No place in time to tell that you're here
No noise no sound not even your breath
No thinking any thoughts there's nothing left
Lost in limbo suspended without mind
Illusion without reality dead and blind

02/02/06

Too Late

I'm dying inside no brain in my
head
I live no more in the land of
the dead
I see no light in this place I'm
in
Condemned to death I die
again and again
No solace from pain I suffer
all the time
I burn to tears covered in
slime
I'm purged for my sins this is
my fate
I'm dying in regret repenting
too late.

4-23-09

Who Am I?

You think you really know me
but with your wildest imaginations
you really don't have a clue
you picture me as evil
with images so untrue
you think you know my ways
as if you could predict
my next move
but just like an illusion
you really do not have a clue
you fear my formless shadow
especially at night
you fear me as a spectacle
as you cower in shameful
fright
you pray for my rebuttal
as if I really care
you even pray to rebuke
my name
as if I were really there
who am I, as if you
have a clue
and who are you
when you believe
that I am separate
from you.

Virtues of a Man

Pardon me and consider other options to your plight
Think it over carefully and make sure you do what's
right
You've made some bad decisions that affect your life
today
But now listen carefully to what I have to say
You'll have a better future if you just turn the
Other cheek
You'll find your life much easier, acting wise and
meek
Show a lot more courtesy and consideration
Be the man that God made you, not just an Imitation
Be a man of righteous cause, who stumbles not in his
ways
Be a man who stands for truth, who humbles himself
and prays
Be a pious and a gentleman, moral and impeccably
sound
Be a brotha to anotha when his head is down
Be a man to your family especially to your father and
Bother, with love for your sisters, with love for
Your brothers, and those who care for each other.
But most of all, be a man with integrity and dignity
when no one's around, your virtues abound,
when no one else can see.

10-18- 07

Light Walkers

We walk as examples
Guiders of the light
We walk through barriers
Using inner sight
We use symbols as
Messages and sometimes
Psalms
We speak for the innocent
To right the wrong
We come from above
As well as below
So we think you have
A right to know
That we are one
Our future is forever
And we are here
And we are together
As guiders of light
And wisdom divine
We lead by example
To instruct mankind
We are light walkers
Guiders of light
We walk by faith
Not by sight

4-25-11

World Peace

Seeking something spiritual, a miracle at the most
Looking for a sign above, a phenomenon of host
I'm praying for a miracle, a sign to set me free
I need some faith from above enough to carry me
I would like to hope and believe, more than just a
wish
That I could write and rephrase my last years
Christmas list
I would put down my pencil and pray to the Lord
And get on my knees and meditate on his Word
I ask not only for my girl and me
But for the whole world to be set free
I pray for the hungry, the homeless, and the poor
I pray for the blind, who can't see no more
I pray for the mute, I pray for the deaf
I pray for the lonely, who have nothing else left
I pray for the mindless, who have lost their soul
I pray for the elders, past sixty years old
I pray for the mighty, I pray for the weak
I pray for the babies, who have yet to speak
But most of all, but none the least
I pray for the love of God to give us world peace

4-04-09

Grant Me Grace

I give myself to you, Lord of Hosts
The Father, the Son, and the Holy Ghost
I surrender in ultimate submission
Bowing in reverence and humble admission
In humility, with no regret
All I have is my life left
So to my God and Lord above
I pledge my allegiance, with loyalty and
love
I question not my keeper's sake
I pray when I am asleep and when I am awake
Lord, bless me and keep me in your care
Keep me from danger and watch me when no
one is there
Give me discernment to make wise decisions
And grant me patience, when it's time to
listen
I pray to the Lord to grant me favor
When my time comes to meet my Maker
And when I meet you, face to face
I pray to God to grant me grace.

2-26-09

A Prayer 1

Gracious Holy Spirit, rain down on
Me, bless me with all the blessings
That I can receive, open my eyes and
Lift me up and bless me with all
Knowledge and wisdom and set my
Feet down on solid ground and give
Wind to my wings while I wear my
Crown, lift me up to the highest
Heavens, and while the music of the
Angels temper my soul, Lord, give
Me the elixir and the nectar of
The gods while I feast at your
Table, the food and wine that
Never cease, and give me the
Eternal radiant fire of eternal
Life, that I may be one with you
Lord, hear my prayer and bless my
name.

2-22-09

A Prayer 2

Down in the dungeons but none the least
crushed by desire but not by defeat
alone in my cell doing my time
I think about nothing but peace of mind
it's just another day and then it will end
alone in my cell with nobody or friends
I read my Bible almost every day
and I talk to the Lord and on my knees I pray
I pray for deliverance, not just from jail
but from boredom in a ten-by-twelve cell
I seek through endurance a peaceful soul
refill my heart that has a painful hole
I pray for faith and I accept God's grace
as I look for myself as I stand in place

I concentrate and meditate as I pray
on God's gift of grace and living this way
I think I can feel it 'cause it seems right
I know and I believe it beyond mortal sight
may God's kingdom come before the twilight night
and release me from this prison like a bird in flight

Psalms from Shaw 2

Precious Lord, please come to me
And help deal with this misery
I need your strength to keep me strong
I need your righteousness when I am wrong
Lift me up when I'm down on my knees
Look past my weakness and forgive me please

3-14-09

Here I am, oh, precious grace
Waiting to see you face to face
I bide my time and wait for you
And ask what you would have me do
I pray O God with your precious grace
To take me with you to your heavenly place

3-14-09

My Father, my God who reigns supreme
Teach me, O God, what you want me to be
Lead me and guide me toward the goal
To the gates of heaven to save my soul
Light my way and lift my burdens
Erase my pain when I am hurtin'
God forgive me and bless me too
And grant me peace when I come to you

3-14-09

My Prayer

My life is hard, every day's a struggle
I get by on my own, but I could use some
Help though
I need a break, something financial
Just enough, nothing special
I ask for nothing just to be free
And a way to provide for my baby and me
Lord, lift me up so I can see
And grant me favor for my baby and me
I need a new life with no remorse
I would like a new house and a car, of
course
I would love to have Inez Taylor as my
wife
So I would have joy and happiness in my
life
If I should die before I wake
I pray the Lord my soul to take.

2-19-09

Lord, Forgive Me

Lord, forgive me for my mistake
And forgive me for promises that I did
make
Lord, forgive me for my words when I
did lie
And forgive me for using false alibis
Lord, forgive me for forsaking you for
worldly love
And forgive me for turning from
heaven above
Lord, forgive me when I was blessed
And I turned and made my life a mess
Lord, forgive me when I denied your
cross
I was foolish and ignorant and
desperately lost
Lord, forgive me when I knew
Like Peter I denied you too
Lord, forgive me for my lack of faith
and losing my way in my haste
Lord, forgive me and grant me pardon
I pray to the Lord, thy will be done.

2-26-09

The One 2

Behold her love is adorned with her beauty,
Her cast that she was molded in is no more!
For perfection has had its final triumph!
The pinnacle of its objective has been reached!
There can be no breach of this action,
And creation is at a standstill, beholding
Its completion of its long-awaited desire!
She is everything that is expected in its
Perfect, true, complete form, for she is
Truth incarnate, she is the "all in all," the
Absolute ideal image of love in human form,
And there will never be another, as
True or pure or holy as she, for she is
The composition of the desired ideal
Of *the one*.

03-20-08

Nyechelle

I have born a baby angel
Of which I am very proud of
Her smile lights up my life
She radiates unconditional love
She's beauty in all its attractions
As love smiles from her eyes
Her charms are blessed and many
Even when she adorably cries
She's my lovable bundle of joy
Whom everyone instantly loves
She thrills the beholding looker
She's all that I think of
She's my baby angel
Sent from heaven above
Given to me a gift adorned
With unconditional baby love
She's a very special baby
Unlike any other
With only one exception
She's special
Like her mother

03-20-08

Nyechelle 2

Have you seen her?
Have you seen her smile?
Have you looked into her eyes?
Does she make you smile?
Does she make you laugh?
Does she warm your heart?
Do you want to hold her?
Do you love her?
So do I.

03-20-08

Love Daddy

I write this poem to my precious
Little angel—Nyechelle Shaw
I love you, my little angel
With all my daddy heart
You are such a pretty baby
So precious and so special to me
You light up my life
I am so proud to be your father
I never thought it would happen
But you made a believer out of me
You were a long time coming
But now you are finally here
I am glad you made it
I promise to you and your mother
That I will always be with you
And be there for you and take
Care of you and always love you
No matter what, in all my daddy
duties, responsibilities, and obligations
With unconditional love.

Love,
Daddy
03-20-08

Soul Sista

Soul sista, soul sista strong in the word
A real Black Panther, haven't you heard
A positive motivator in the community
Always around when a friend's in need
She speaks her mind, holding nothing back
She growls like a panther before she attacks
But she's gentle as a lamb, as sweet as can be
But don't underestimate her, listen to me
She stands up for her principles, you better believe
She's a winner, a charmer, as cool as can be
She's on a mission, she's all about it, that's how she gets down
So if you want to know how she flows, don't act like a clown
'Cause she's a woman, like no other, rare and unique
Her words are wise that gratify everyone she meets
Her name is Michelle, she's fine as well, as a matter of fact
Beauty and brains are her claim to fame, there's nothing that
she lacks
I treasure her friendship, it's genuine, and she feels the same
She's a soldier and a real soul sista—*Michelle Autry* is her
name

12/ 11/ 07

Brianna

You are a beautiful rose without the thorns
You are immaculate, and pure from the day you
were born
You are the glory and honor of your mother's
heart
Your gracefulness and charms set you apart
From all the others who stand in the presence of
your radiance
And you too are my pride and joy as you are my
princess
So cheers to you and all that you do
For all the sunshine and brilliance that is you
You are the star, the apple of your mother's eye
And you will always shine like the stars in the sky
Your preciousness makes you worth more than gold
For you are beautiful, you know it, so let it show
The world is waiting for your diamond to shine
So sing and dance to the rhythm and rhyme
Be free, Brianna, and express yourself
Don't worry about trying to please anyone else
Just be happy and do your thing
And you will find what happiness and love will
bring
It will bring you joy and freedom from despair
And you will find comfort and peace from there

6-14-09

Well Done

Cheers to you, my sister
for all the good you do
you raised up a Trojan
and a saint was given
to you
for all it's worth
for pain and glory
the world will
pronounce yours
and his story
for together with pride
you both have come
through trials and tribulations
with honors and fame
and so to you, my sister
I write this dedication
with pride and joy
and admirable adulation
I hope with prayer
that you'll continue your quest
to seek
your peace
until you find rest
God bless you and keep you
for many years to come
find peace and comfort
for a job well-done.

Beloved

Beloved of God, mother of the earth
May God grant you grace for all its worth
And bless you with bounty beyond your
dreams
And open up the heavens so you will know
what it means
To be with God in his heavenly place
And shine like the sun when you look in his
face
And find comfort and solace and peace and
rest
And abide in God in his heavenly nest
May the peace of God rest in your soul
And bring you comfort when you get old
May love surround you in your time of need
May the grace of his word plant its seed
In your heart and mind that you continue to
believe
And follow in his footsteps and you will
surely see
That he was and is always with you
Beloved of God, these words are true

5-12-09

Oprah

I'd like to give special mention
To someone whom I admire and adore
I'd like to express my gratitude
To someone who means so much more
She's a special kind of woman
A lighthouse of guiding light
Her star shines above in the heavens
A diamond pearl in the moonlit night
She's patient with love and compassion
She's generous with her time
She speaks with heartfelt passion
She swoons the passive mind
I long to be in her presence
Just to have her close to me
And hug and tell her I love her
A dream, a fantasy
I know that I'll be searching
Trying to find some way
To meet my *idol Oprah*
May God speed the day.

1/22/06

Michael Jackson

Here's to Michael Jackson
whose fame framed his name
his brilliant talent in the
world of entertainment
sealed a clause that none could claim
a genius in his own right
unlike any other
loved by all, adored by all, especially
his sisters and brothers
he was a man who loved to
dance and sing to the crowd
he was the best, excepting nothing less
he made his family proud
there will never be another
Michael Jackson
no, not in a million years
many have tried, and all have failed
he left the world in tears
to all the Michael Jackson fans
whose music plays on in their hearts
remember Michael's love for you
and his memory will always be part
of your lives as you dance and sing
to "Thriller" and "Billie Jean,"
remember the times he made you laugh
and filled the world with dreams.

Sky and Angel

I have two very special angels
Sent from heaven up above
Their names are Sky and Angel
My two little girls that I love
They keep me very busy
And it's fun all the time
We laugh a lot and party
I think of them all the time
Their mother's a real jewel
Whom they love and adore
She's a special kind of woman
What child could ask for more?
I love my little family
Although they're not really mine
We have a beautiful relationship
That's wonderfully one of a kind
Angel is shy and beautiful
She's really quiet and sweet
While Sky is just the opposite
She's beautiful and loves to speak
They're both unique and lovely
Although different I love them just the same
I love them both no differently
Sky and Angel are their names

Love,
Uncle Billy
1/22/06

A *Bee's* Story

I am a bee that flies above trees
Flying in the wind that carries me
Looking for honey, I go from flower to flower
Sometimes I find some that are bitter and sour
But usually I am correct, and I find a real sweet one
And I suck it up and won't leave till I'm done
I and my fellows constantly stay busy
We move so fast and bump heads and get dizzy
As a bee, I stop and think
Why is the sky blue and not pink?
You may think it odd that a bee can think
But there's something else strange, why do skunks stink?
Yes, I am a wonder as I buzz on by
Thinking how I'd like to have a bite of your cherry pie
Do not be mad when you see us flying in the air
But just in case you do, ask me ask me if I care
I have a job, when I'm done I'll head home
I don't have the luxury of a mankind who struggles and roam
If you want my opinion or just my advice
Stay away from hungry bears, they ain't nothin' nice
Raccoons are greedy, they just can't get enough
I'd like to sting them dead and have them all stuffed
These are just my opinions, heed them if you will
If you were a bee, you'd know how I feel
But you are a man, and read these little lines
And if you think I'm funny, then that's just fine
'Cause next time I see you, I'll sting your fat behind

05-14-96

Water

You need me and you know it
And you really don't have to say
Because you use me fickly
At least twice a day
You drink your coffee and soda pop
And sometimes some kinda juice
You neglect me even now
I feel I have little use
When you are thirsty
I quench your hungry thirst
But you drink a soda pop
When I should be really first
How could you survive
How could you live
If not for the water
For the sustenance I do give
So next time you're thirsty
Think of this little rhyme
Drink a lot of water
It cools the body and mind.

08/18/97

The Dragon

Way up high on a mountaintop a
Dragon perches on his throne
Wondering if there are others
Wondering if it is alone
It looks in the distance seeing
What it can see
Far above the lofty clouds far
Above the forest trees it roars
Out loud in a high-pitched scream
Spreading its wings to fly it takes
To the air in full display flying
Higher than high
There flies the dragon majestic
And alone
It seeks its own kind far from its
Lofty home
It looks for another to share its
Throne
But for now while in flight it
Roams the sky alone.

7-24-09

The Dragon 2

Far above the lofty hills way up in the
clouds
The dragon sleeps in his cave snoring
Out so loud
It dreams of days far gone by when
Paradise did reign
When dragons ruled when dragons played
And dragons had their way
Now paradise lost the future forgone
And tomorrows dimmed in gloom
The dragon's reign now memories pain and
Demise filled with doom
For dragons today in iniquities' way are
Mythical as of the past
For legends are made with future intents
But the memories never last
So the dragon sleeps with memory it weeps
It dreams of yesterdays
But tomorrow it will awake and make its
Stake being a dragon in every way
It will take its place upon its throne high
Up past the hills
And spread its wings and blow its flames and
Roar and holler and shrill
And soar through the air way up high far
Above the lofty hills

7-28-09

Consequences

Confronted with indecision
Trying to do what's right
Thinking about the reasons
That makes my darkness
bright
A peculiar urge disturbs me
Unsettling at the most
I foresee a future unrest
Full of angry ghosts
Consequences abound me
Telling me what to do
I want to do the right thing
But is the right thing
Always the
Option for who?

2-05-09

Limerick

I'm practically, immaculately, impossibly sound. I'm intelligently, relatively, impeccably round. I'm thoroughly, socially, disturabably down. I'm evenly, so believe in me when I'm around. So you see, even if we never knew how, there would be, or never be, eternity now. So try to receive and retrieve what we could be, if you yearn and you learn your ABCs. By the way, if I say something you like, get a pen, write a check, and send it to Mike. Take your time, ease my mind, and let me unwind. Check the weather with a feather then rewind. My promiscuity is socially unaccepted by most, but I hear they are profiling me as I rascuelly boast. I drink my wine, tip my hat, and give them a toast; give them the finger and disappear like a ghost.

12/11/07

Mr. Majestic

Defined as I am
I am majestic at best
I am brilliantly awesomely none
Like the rest
I am no match for you attached to
You I must confess
I try to be humbly nobolly less
Thankfully willfully I am blatantly
true
When it comes to me talking to you
Ask of me when will we intimately
Get down
I will let you know as before when I
Come around
So come to me lustfully and let's
Have some fun
And I will repeatedly sexually
Make you cum.

2-13-09

Doing Time

Suspended in animation doing time in a cell
Stuck in this cycle, in and out of jail
Avoiding the feelings that I have rejected in
The past
Like being hurt and lonely, hoping they
Don't last
The days go by so slowly I am trying to
Ignore the time
Trying to be patient but it stays on my mind
I wish I would get some mail so I would know
Someone cares
But just like ghost no one is really there
I work out to stay fit and write some poetry
Wondering if someone somewhere is
Missing me
I think about a lot of things reminiscing on
The past
I think about how much I miss it but nothing
Good ever lasts
My times go by heavy on my mind
Hoping for release that will never come on
Time
So here I sit in animated suspension
Waiting to be sent upstate to prison

2-17-09

Reminiscing

They have me in a prison, confined to a cell
It's called the dungeons, the closest thing to
Hell
I use memories and imagination to deal with
The time
So I talk to my celly, to get it off my mind
I think about the memories of the good
Times I've had
Some weren't so good, but then they all
Weren't so bad
I mostly miss my baby, Nyechelle Nicole Shaw
I wish I had a telephone so that I could call
And hear her sweet angelic voice once more
Because it's her beautiful innocence that I
Really adore
She's my only child that I will ever love
A beautiful angel sent from heaven above
Confined to this cell, a dungeon, a prison
I have a story to tell, but who's gonna listen
The confinement alone can drive you insane
And the memories added increase the pain
Remorse and regret are my only friends
Thinking about my mistakes and what could
Have been
So much to think about and so much time
I try to be positive to ease my mind
I think about the future and what could be
And imagine life with my baby and me
I would have a big house with just one car
And I would take my baby to Hollywood and

Make her a star
She would have the best things that money
Could buy
And I love and care for her until the day I
Die
These are some of the things I plan to do
With me and my baby, with just us two
I also reminisce and think about the past
And think about how time goes by so fast
All those moments and chances I've had
I should have went home, but now I've lost my
Pad
I could have avoided the whole situation
If I had chosen to leave without hesitation
But what the hell, no time for regrets
I have to move on, with the time I have left
Confined in this prison, locked in a cell
Hoping one day to be released from this hell

3-09-09

Man Up

Trapped in this prison behind these cold
Stone walls
Locked up for years, no one to call
All I do is think all day
At night I dream the day away
Time is on my side, locked within
It's hard to do, but then again
I got time to do, I just can't win
When will it end, about a year or so
But where I will end up, I don't know
Will I survive while my life is at stake
I pray to the Lord, my soul to take
If I should die before I awake
Ain't no security in this life I am in
You got to watch your enemies and your
Friends
I am in this prison, it ain't nothing new
What seems right could be wrong to you
The rules are different behind these walls
They may save your life or end it all
There is no redemption or rehabilitation
You better pray to God for your salvation
It's a cold dark world in a prison institution
You better man up and make a resolution
To do this time, and don't let it do you
And make your peace with God, and maybe
You will make it through.

2-19-09

Prisoner of Time

Looking at time from the inside
A prisoner of time that has me bound
By no chains, fences, or bars
I'm bound in prison by time
Its monotonous, ceaseless routine
cycle
Has me in its grip like King Kong
I can't fight or resist its hold on me
It doesn't make sense, it doesn't care
It doesn't talk, it doesn't walk
It doesn't sleep nor does it eat
It could care less about my tears of
fear
It cannot sympathize with my pain or
sorrow
This time is a muthafucka, man
It ain't no joke, ain't nothing to be
played with
And my only recourse and advice to
you
Is to let time go and let it be
And you find the secret of time's
Hold on you is that you believe it.

3-26-09

Finally Find Some Peace

Locked in this prison, locked in this cell
Locked in this dungeon, locked in this hell
With nothing to do, but do this time
Time goes by, but it stays on my mind
When will it stop, when will it cease
I need some peace or early release
I'm tired all the day, and I sleep all night
Confined in the darkness, seeking the light
Thinking about the future and what could
be
Thinking about my life, was this meant for
me
I'm living for the future while dying to the
past
I'm presently in expectancy, hoping time goes
by fast
Trying to be positive, optimistic at the most
I hope I'm not too confident, don't want to
brag or boast
I like the thought that I beat my time and
will be called for early release
That I would soon go home and be with my
family and finally find some peace

4-03-09

They Took My Freedom

They took my freedom
And put me in an institution
They took my freedom
And made me pay restitution
They took my freedom
And locked me in a cell
They took my freedom
And put me through hell
They took my freedom
By stalling my time
They took my freedom
By trying to stop my mind
They took my freedom
So I will have no choice
They took my freedom
So I will have no voice
They took my freedom
So I will have no place to live
They took my freedom
So I will have nothing to give
They took my freedom
And denied my rights
They took my freedom
And stopped my life
They took my freedom
But they can't keep me.

12-25-09

Grieving

I live with grief, alone all the time
I'm trying to stay sane, but I'm losing
my mind
Condemned by a crime, that ain't my
fault
Convicted to live in a prison vault
Will I survive this human tragedy
Or will I die, never to be free
My only thought is my little family
My girl, my baby, and me
I pray to God to set me free
Back to the life with my baby girl
and me

4-23-09

No Justice

God, forgive me for my lack of faith
I'm getting beat down by the year 2008
With the odds against me, my back is to the wall
Too many enemies, I'm about to fall
Lord, have mercy and lend me a hand
Taking too many blows for just one man
Stuck in society, can't get no wealth
The only thing I got is good health
Ain't got no money, with bills to pay
So I walk these streets every day
Looking for a job to heal these ills
And buy me a house and pay these bills
Time's running out, I'm getting older
Got the weight of the world on these shoulders
I see no light in the future ahead
I'd like to be rich before I'm dead
Got chains in my life, in a jail of sorts
Imprisoned by the laws that abuse me for sport
Can't get no justice, there is no peace
Sentenced to time with no release
Looking for an avenue, but there's no way out
I'd like to win the lottery, now that's what I'm talking about.

1-28-08

My Memoirs

I've lived a fucked-up life for forty-six years
Been neglected and rejected and still refuse to shed tears
Can't say it's not been all my fault
But I did what I could with what I was taught
Got a bad disposition, don't trust anybody
My past ain't shit, my future looks shoddy
Got a few ideas, gotta few dreams
I'd like to express myself, If you know what I mean
Write some poetry, write some raps
Write some song lyrics, tip or taps
Gotta get past my overbearing past
If I am to succeed, I have to act fast
Shit keeps happening, getting in my way
Gotta stay positive, getting past today
Can't go down, can't give up
Can't give in, and don't give a fuck
Don't have no hang-ups, no regrets
I'm gonna give it my all, on that you can bet!

1-17-07

Keep It Real

Don't be phony
Don't be a prude
Don't be stupid
Don't be rude
You don't have to act
Like something you're not
Don't act like a thug
And get yourself shot
There are some shady
Individuals
Who you just can't trust
They talk a lot of trash
But end up eatin' the dust
So to all the real homies
A word to the few
Keep your head up, brotha
'Cause cowards do what
They have to
But players know what to do.

03-30-06

Thank You

Thank you for your patience
Thank you for your time
Thank you for giving me
Peace of mind
I want you to know
That the time we spent
I want you to know
How much it meant
You gave me so much confidence
You dispelled my doubts
And all my nonsense
I know I can't repay you
For all you have done
So I'd like to let you know
That I love you, my father
From your son

8-16-97

The Rain 1

Ain't shed no tears, ain't ready to cry
My eyes stayed dry when my mama died
Neither shed a tear when my girlfriend lied
Really can't remember crying any tears
It's been so long, so many years
I ain't so hard, I feel some pain
But it ain't deep enough to cause the rain
Empathy, sympathy, I feel your pain
But still it's not enough to bring the rain
Feeling so emotional, sometimes grieves me
But it's not enough to start the rain
I have enough love to have compassion
Still no tears to start the rain
Trials and tribulations surround me
But it's not enough to bring the rain
Sometimes I'm ecstatic, high on life
My eyes stay dry, no use for rain
My eyes still show disdain
My contempt and disdain for the rain is maybe
I haven't found enough love or pain
To bring forth this rain

11-20-07

Just Like Me

Down in the gutter, beat by defeat
I lay on the pavement on the cold
street
Intoxicated with wine and beer in hand
I cry to myself, feeling less than a man
My behavior is erratic, I am destitute
and broke
I am dying inside, I am losing all hope
Nobody cares about me, so why should I?
I am just a statistic, who cares if I die?
Here I am, a shell of a man
If God can't help me, then who the hell
can?
To the depths of hell is were I am going
When my heart stops beating and my
blood stops flowing
I am a pitiful sight, don't look at me
I don't want your pity, can't you see?
There is a whole lot of people who
look just like me

2-13-09

Safer Cities Initiative

Safer Cities Initiative—who's it for?
Safe for the rich, dangerous for the poor
They say it's good, but not for me
As far as they're concerned, I'm the enemy
They prowl the streets, looking for me
They pervert the law to please the city
Who are they, the police, the Gestapo, the KGB?
They want me out of the way to impose the laws
But their instigation will be their fall
I'm not gonna stand for it, only to run
Giving the pig an opportunity to use his gun
They harass me to intimidate me, to invoke the
law
They want me off the streets, but that's not all
They'd like to put me in a prison to shut my
mouth
But imma keep on talking, let me scream and
shout
Get up, stand up, and stand up for your rights
Let's get down, now's the time to fight
Know your rights and protect your freedom
SCI—we don't need 'em.

9/19/08

I Wish She Were Mine

I met a girl whose
Beauty is profound
Whose words are melodies,
Such beautiful sounds
Grace carries her gently,
As she goes about her way
Visions of her beauty
Fills my mind night and day
Love is a gift
And thus she gives
And love is truth
And for this she lives
What more can a man
Ask for in a woman so fine.
What more you say?
I wish she were mine.

03/28/96

The Game

You are so beautiful
My mind is in a bind
I cannot seem to get
You out of my mind
Why do I have these feelings
That I cannot seem to express
I believe your eyes are asking me
To take some kind of test
If this is your desire
If this is your request
If for your love that I shall win
I'll truly do my best
For want of your love
Appease me
Your secrets are my spell
For you are truly beautiful
In truth I tell no tale
I ponder as I write these lines
What wonders will love reveal
What mysteries will be truly answered
As to my lover's zeal
I cheer to your passion
For the game that you play
I smile and think to myself
I would have it no other way
What gift does love hide from me
I know it will be worth the find
I know I'll find the answer
And make you mine all mine.

8-24-97

The Pursuit

Your demeanor hides a veil to the unknown
For I see you, but I do not know you
Your essence is hidden behind your eyes
I love you, but I am not sure
If you will be receptive to my advances
For I sense a screen, a facade of a person
I am inclined to be a fool
And I approach you with apprehension
But indecision stalls my initiative
Compelled by my need to know
I pursue on, thinking only of folly
For the object of my desire
Is a quest I've longed for
So I go in pursuit of the unknown
I wonder will I be received with interest
Or will I be denied with shameful
embarrassment
Finally impulse compels me
And I approach you with warning
I come to you, and I speak to you
And you smile and respond with a pleasant
hello
The veil was lifted, the unknown is no more
We talked like old friends, you are
absolutely beautiful
And I was thinking what was I so worried
about.

6-08-09

I Wish

I heard your voice again; it woke me up. I couldn't help myself. I was just lying down, trying to fall asleep. I got up and wrote this poem down because that's the kind of effect you have on me. I can't resist you. I am powerless around you, and in reality, I do not want to resist you. You have a power and a persuasion over me as if I am hypnotized when I know you are near. I get anxious and excited. I only wish you could know how I feel about you; I wish you could know how you make me feel. I wish you could know how much power you have over me. I wish . . .

10/18/07

Your Face

The first time I saw your face
My heart started beating at a rapid pace
Inside it felt very funny, and I couldn't explain why
As the light shined in your dreamy brown eyes
So I reached out to touch you and made contact
With your hand
Then I whisper into your ear, do you have a man
'Cause I think for sure he shouldn't have left you
alone
If I had it my way I'd take you straight home
Double lock the door, throw away the key
Take my time with you and grant you all of me
Rub you starting from your feet to your head
You would feel so extra special as you visit my bed
However, just when you thought it was over, I
Crack open some wine
Suck and lick your entire body within an hour's
time
Do things to your body that you never dreamed
Rub you down with hot oils and break out the
Whipped cream
I should have informed you that you were in for a
treat
In the background, sounds flowing to a mellow
beat

Our bodies were locked together, one of the same
As we lay in the bed and exchanged nicknames
Your lips are so shiny; can I have a taste?
Would you believe it all started with one look at
your face.

12-03-09

At Last

Falling in love as I kiss you
again
My mind starts to drift to way
back when
Back to a memory a time long
ago
Back down the lane to someone I
know
She was a diamond, a jewel from
the earth
Precious and sweet and divine
since birth
I love her from that time until
memory past
I now found her love before me
at last.

5-02-09

Our Love

My one true *love* I cannot deny
I *love* you more than ever
Until the day I die
More than feelings or physical attraction
It's your sincerity and selflessness
That define your action
Your grace and beauty consume my *soul*
Your *words* are music that make me whole
We are *one* of the same spirit
You and I
Our destinies are bound together
And here's the reason why
Our *love* for each other
Is of *pure* mind
We are *one* of another
With thoughts divine
Our motives and intentions
Are *one* and the *same*
We are *truth* and understanding
Without any games
I am *love*, in *love* with you
For your *love* eternally *true*

6-25-11

Make You Mine

I am centrically, intellectually, impeccably unique. I'm artistically, articulately profound when I speak. I object fully, willfully, absolutely stand my ground. I'm agreeable, tactfully, socially sound. Don't blatantly, disrespectfully put me down, or I'll arguably debate, fully make a sound. I am not sarcastic or uppity, if that's what you think. I'm peacefully, tranquilly, serene-fully in sync. I'm thoughtfully, carefully, considerably true. I'm ecstatically, delightfully attracted to you. If you are wondering or pondering what to say, don't hesitantly speak you see, give it a day. I don't want you to feel you, have to respond. Just think about it, write about it, but we'll still get along. I just want to say, about today, I think you're divine, and if I could, I would, or should, make you mine.

12/ 28/ 07

Imagination

Am I being tested? I wonder! Do you look at me the way I think you do? Or is it just my imagination? I keep saying to myself "naw," it couldn't be true, but what if? Just what if? Imagine that—that you could be thinking of me the same way too! Is this a test? Are you playing mind games with me? Maybe I'm just fooling myself into thinking maybe you want me the same way I want you! What if? "Naw," it couldn't be, but I'd like to think of what could be. If only you had an imagination just like me.

10/18/07

What Am I to Do?

How much can I tell you
How much do I reveal
How much can I trust you
Are you really real
How can I show you
Can you be really true
Can I tell you I love you
Just what am I to do
How do I come
Am I first or last
Where do I stand
I'm kinda confused
Do I speak or whisper
Or do I make a scene
If I do, should I come clean
Do I stand a chance
Will you let me know
Do I wait and stand by, or do I let go.

04-30-96

The Eyes Never Lie

When I look into your eyes
There's a mirror that I see
I see a reflection of myself
An image imagining me
I feel a love-rooted passion
In the core of my soul
For your eyes reveal
Your love
That only you can know
I see a vision in your eyes
A mystery known to me
I see a light in your eyes
Of love's desire for me
I feel a fire in my soul
When I look into your eyes
Like a burning inferno inside me
That burns my heart inside
I know my woman loves me
I see it in her eyes
I know she loves me intimately
'Cause the eyes never lie.

1/15/05

Be Mine

I saw you from a distance
Not too long ago
I saw you with eyes
That only my mind knows
I saw you in a vision
In a mirror in my mind
I saw you from a distance
In a place across time
I knew you were coming
It was more than a dream
I ponder this revelation
And imagine what it means
I hope you do not mind
I want you to know that my love for you
Has spanned the space of time
So without insistence, now is the time
I am asking you to marry me
Please please be mine.

1/15/05

In My Dreams

I was awakened last night in the midst of my dream
There was a mellow feeling, somewhat like ice cream
I was stuck in a situation I didn't want to end
I was Adam, you were Eve, the apple was the sin
We both tiptoed through the garden to avoid the thorns
Both not wanting our hearts to be torn
I thought I had control of the situation, or so it seemed
But you're the first person I allowed to invade my dreams
Since I think about you so much, and you know it's true
Give me action at one of your dreams, and see what I can do
I will creep into your bed, removing all your clothes
I will massage your entire body, even your pretty toes
You will reach for my body as you become so wet
I remember you being that way the first time we had sex
Now you're fighting with the sheets and end up on the
floor
Screaming my name, begging me for more
You're running out of breath as you witness my power
And your fingers have been stuck in the same position for
over an hour
You're at that point now to where you're gonna cum
You begin to shake uncontrollably, and your body becomes
so numb
Now that you're relaxed and feeling so free without a
care
Just to awaken alone and realize that no one's there
You wonder how could this be, when your eyes still hold
that gleam
Well, it's just payback, love, for invading in on my dreams.

12-03-09

Sacred Chambers

I have the key to unlock your heart,
The secret mystery to your love gate.
I have found your sacred chambers.
Hidden beneath the dew that covers
Your spring, the fountain of eternal
Life, I know the passion that awaits
Me, as I proceed to unlock your
Treasure chest, but I hesitate and
Ponder the outcome of my decision,
Will I open your treasure chest and be
Met with the aroma of ecstasy with
Sweet euphoria, or will I open Pandora's
Box and be intoxicated with the vilest
Of evils and death, whatever the
Outcome I accept because I am blind to
Your beauty, and I am willing to die,
Just for one chance at making love to
You, for just one night. And so I enter
The key into your sacred chambers, and
Your love gate opens, and I am not
Disappointed.

2-12-09

Divine Love

I saw you as you saw me all alone on that quiet night. It was an intimate moment as the moon reflected your light, the light that sparkles from your eyes that reveal your secrets within, the thoughts of love and intimacy, the love from a woman to a man. I remember that night so thoughtfully as if it happened today. I know I'll never forget it, for mere words cannot say, for you are so fine—an image of mine, a sweet mirage, a vision of sunshine. True beauty is priceless, more precious than gold. Your beauty is spiritual, a sight to behold. Such radiant beauty, brilliant from within, a gift of such glory. On my knees I bend to your grace and purity. My angel from above, I write this poem with supreme adulation and divine love.

10/ 07 /07

Two Beautiful Butterflies

The sky is ours in the starlit night as we chase the wind in butterfly flight. As melodies from the heavens twinkle with delight, as the moon glow beams and pursues our flight. The sparkle of love whispers through the night about the two beautiful butterflies who found love in the night.

10/18/07

I Want You

I want to lay you down and make
love to you
I want to take off your clothes and
massage, rub you down
I want to touch every part of your
body as I oil you down
I want to hear you moan as you
breath in ecstasy
I want to feel your heat as my
fingers probe your body
I want to feel your nipples harden
as I fondle your breast
I want to feel the moisture between
your legs
I want your tender love all night.
As we make love,
I want you to feel me.
I want you.

2-8-2010

I Love You 1

I love you now, I love you later
I'll love you through time for now, forever
I love you without reason, unconditionally
I love you for your love that overwhelms me
I love in the day and through the night
I love you 'cause your smile makes it all right
Your sweetness radiates from within without
With the body of a goddess that makes the angels shout
I love your eyes that sparkle and shine
I love to hold your fine body close to mine
The sweetness of your kiss makes me say
I want you in my arms every single day
I love to hear your voice, a song to my heart
I long just to hear it, every minute were apart
I love to hear your moan, a lovely echo in my mind
When we make love, when your body's under mine
This letter is to my love, my heart's desire
'Cause you are so fine, you set my soul on fire
I'm sprung on your love, and I want more
You got your hooks in me, down to the core
I'm not ashamed to say that you make me weak
Every time I see you, my knees buckle, I can't speak
What words could describe you, what language do I use
Should I sing it in a song, or do I write it in a muse
Your love is beyond glory, brighter than the sun
I love you 'cause you're special, girl, you're the one!

05-22-96

I Love You 2

I love you without reason
'cause you're one of a kind
I love you 'cause you're beautiful
you're always on my mind
I love your passion
you're beautiful inside
your words are like music
that fills my lonely nights
I've fallen so deeply
in love with you, I love it when you're
with me
because your love is
so true
I love your beautiful smile
that makes your face shine
your eyes sparkle like diamonds
I'm so glad you're mine
I dedicate these words
of love from me to you
'cause you mean the world
to me, 'cause your love is
so true.
I love you.

I Love You 3

I love you 'cause you're lovely
I wonder what else it could be
you're special and adorable
and you raise my family
so I thank you from my heart
with the precious love we share
and I hope that for God's sake
that you will always be there
thank you for my family
and for all the love and care
and for all the time you've taken
while I am not there
I love you more than anything
and I thank you from my heart
and I love you for my babies
although we're far apart.
I love you.

Love Letter 1

I remember you in so many ways.
Your beauty is esoteric, beyond words.
It is love in its purest form, richer
And more valuable than diamonds. You
Are perfect, like an angel from heaven, as
Fine and refined as the purest gold
And as divine as divine holy grace.
Mere words cannot describe you.
You belong to me only; I desire nothing more
In life than to have you for myself.
You possess my heart and soul; I need you by
My side. You complete me; you fulfill my
Every desire with passion that consumes
All reason.
I love you as myself; we are one person.
Created as one, there is no distance too far
Nor time in eternity that can separate us.
I am you, and you are me; I love you intimately
With all my being; our lives are intricately tangible.
Your voice express my very thoughts; I feel you
And know you as myself; I am totally and absolutely
In love with you.
I share these thoughts with you because I know that
Beyond any doubt you understand and know
And believe exactly as I that our love is beyond
Emotions and feelings. Our love for each other is
Divine love.

Love always,
Billy Shaw

1/30/2006

Love Letter 2

I dream about you. I think about you.
I talk about you, but I can't see you.
I really do not know anything about you.
I do not even know where you are,
even considering that we were actually
quite intimate for one night.
You touched me like no other woman
has ever done in my life. I swear
my feelings for you after that night
has intensified beyond my imagination.
It is an experience that I will always treasure.
I truly look for more from you.
You are so unique, and it was a pleasure
to have your beautiful, lovely naked body
next to mine. I was so thrilled and moved
by your passion. It was pure ecstasy.
I cannot remember at any time in my
natural life, wanting any woman in this
world more than I want you now.
Having your beautiful, luscious, curvaceous naked body
Next to mine was heaven.
I am honored and flattered, and I am very
Privileged that you chose me as your first lover
and companion. You changed my life. I want you.
I need you, and I absolutely have fallen in love with you.

02-02-06

Love Letter 3

What you mean to me could never be expressed fully in words because I love you more than feelings can express, more than emotions or sentiment. Mere words can hardly describe how I feel about you because I love you so intimately, that ultimately I am consumed as well as overwhelmed by hot passion, just standing near the shadow of your frame. You delight me every time I see you. When I finally see you, I have erotic, pornographic thoughts that entice my physical senses to oblivious explosions of immense magnitudes that cause me waves, rapture of intense pleasure throughout, and in my body and mind, that's how much I love you, and this is what you do to me, and I am not ashamed at all because this is my reaction every time I see you, and I just want you to know exactly how you make me feel, and I hope by some strange coincidence that you also have and share the same feelings as I have for you and that our love for each other is mutual and that you will always be my forever lover, always and forever.

A Love Letter

Your smile tells me all I need to know; the sparkle and twinkle in your beautiful eyes radiate your brilliance that illuminates the pure unconditional love that comes from your lovely heart. I am totally and absolutely mesmerized by the person that is you. You inspire me to write poetry of love and intimate passion of the purest form. So I write this poem inspired by you, dedicating these words to your love and all that you are.

10/ 07/ 07

Julie

Julie, Julie with diamonds eyes
like hidden treasure a pure surprise
more beautiful than rubies
more precious than gold
Julie's a real jewel
let her story be told
she's a sweet as honey
as bees can confirm
she's as delicate as a flower
as her sensual soul yearns
for sensual passions
of pleasurable delights
her passion's on fire
like love in the night
Julie's a wonder, like a beautiful dove
that flies alone, looking for love
like a bee, flying from flower to flower
she finds some sweet
she finds some sour
but she remains beautiful
through thick and thin
and no matter what happens
we will always be friends

Imagine That

Hello, sweetheart, here's another
letter from me
I was just thinking of how
sweet it could be
if I could take your hand and ask you to marry me
'cause I've been thinking
and contemplating
wondering if I should
keep you waiting
it's just a thought
that has crossed my mind
but I keep on thinking
it's not the right time
and so I wonder with
thoughts of you
and imagine thoughts
of loving you
you have a pleasing personality
that a lot of women do not possess
you are so beautiful and fine
I must confess
your words of comfort and solace
are spoken with grace
for you are pure love
that shines on your face
a wretch am I unworthy
of your love
and I pray to the heavens
to the Lord above
to be content with just

being your friend
and hope to one day
for your love that
I will win.
Imagine that!

Love Poems

I love it when you love me
when you hold me so close
I love it when you kiss me
I have to brag and boast
I love it when you tell me
that I am your lover man
I love it when you whisper
that no one else can
Love you like I love you
Love to love you baby
For all the good you do
Love to love you sweetheart
Always and forever
From me to you.

To my angel baby
I send my love to you
and I hope beyond a doubt
that you will love me too
I wish I could love you
although you are so far
I wish upon a star my love
to be wherever you are.

Dedicated to You

Hello my precious Gladys
here's a poem for you
for you are all that
and you're beautiful too
to you I dedicate my life
to a life so beautiful and true
with sweet adoration
I give all my love to you.
Why do I love you?
Let me count the ways
you're smart and so articulate
you brighten my lonely days
your smile makes a rainy day
shine so bright
you radiate a love so deep
you keep me up all night
you're a goddess in disguise
come to me from afar
the twinkle in your beautiful eyes
tells me that you are a star.
So what can I say to my
Angel from up above
all I can say from my heart
Thank you God with love

Until the End of Time

Hello, pretty lady, and how do you do
I'm writing this letter, thinking of you
I miss you so much, you stay on my mind
I'm trying to write the right words
so here's another line
you're sweet as honey, and I am the bee
I desire your taste, that's so sweet to me
you're beautiful and exotic and fine as wine
and I can't wait to get you to make you mine
give me all your loving, and I'll give you mine
and I'll bless you forever
until the end of time

Do You
Remember

Hello, angel baby, and how do you do?
I'm writing you this letter,
trying to get close to you
I hope that you receive it with gladness of heart
so I can close this little gap that has set us apart.
What's up with you, are you okay
I hope this little letter
makes you smile all day
I've been thinking about you lately
with the fondest memories
thinking about the times
when you were next to me
maybe I'm just imagining it
but it's heavy on my mind
but I sit still and reminisce
on how you were so fine
do you remember how we
used to talk
we stayed on the phone from
dawn till dark
do you remember when we fell in love
we were very young
like two turtle doves
I remember holding hands
we were close together
like pebbles and sand

and I wonder if you think at all
about the time we made love
in the fall
remember the time we fell in love
we were young and innocent then
do you remember after all
I still love you more than friends
and I hope you remember
and never forget
that we were once lovers
and I have not regrets
so I love you, angel baby
and this is how I feel
and I want you to know
that my love for you is real

My Best Friend

We got married on March 1, 2010
when our lives were united
and I married my best friend
you made me so happy
when you took my hand
you were made to be my wife
and I married my best friend
you proved you loved me
from beginning to end
you make me so proud
and I married my best friend
we were meant to be together
and our love will never end
and I'll never love another
because I married my best friend

Dedicated to Gladys

Hello, little darlin'
here's a poem for you
for all the beautiful
things you are and
all the beautiful things you do
you are sweet like honey
you smell like roses in bloom
you're fine as you want to be
I left you too soon.
But I made a promise
and I will be back if it takes forever
and that's a fact.
So to you, my lovely lady
I write this poem for you
because I think you're wonderful
and I think you're beautiful
and also awesome too.
Here's to you, my lady
I dedicate these lines to you
because you are absolutely beautiful
and I am totally in love with you
you are the best thing that has ever happened to me
and I miss you more and more each and every day.
There is not a day that
goes by when you are
not on my mind
I hope and pray that
the feelings that I share with you are mutual
Because I am feeling you
every moment of the day.

Every time we talk on the phone
I listen to your voice
and I am mesmerized
by the soft tone of you.

My Love Is Real

I look at your picture
practically every day
and I love you more
than ever, in a very
special way
I pray to God
in heaven
that you will always
be by my side
even when I stumble
in my foolish pride
I hope that you will
continue to love me
as we go through
the good and the bad
'cause I am willing to
carry you, even when
you're sad
So I write this little
poem
to express to you how
I feel
and I hope that you
will like it
because my love is
real.

Mere Words

How much more can I love you
let me count the ways
first of all you're beautiful
more than words can say
you're sophisticated and eloquent
and wise as you can be
you're the epitome of love
and radiant for all to see
your eyes sparkle and shine
like diamonds in the sky
and when you smile and laugh
I just look at you and sigh
you're more than a woman
priceless more than can be worth
for your worth is beyond comprehension
like nothing found on this earth
you are a goddess set in the
starry heavens above
so wonderful and beautiful
for all to adore and love
what more can I say or do
to describe your adorable ways
if mere words were to define your
beautiful ways
then it's words I'll have
to convey.

To My Children

To my precious adorable children
whom I love with all my daddy heart
you all are very special to me
and nothing can keep us apart
I love you from the sunrise
to the setting of the sun
I love you for all the seasons
until the seasons are done
and I thank you
because you are gifts
from heaven sent from above
with all my daddy intentions
with heartfelt spiritual love
so to my adorable children
I send you peace and love
with many hugs and kisses
with love from God above.

Happy
Birthday

Happy birthday, baby, with the fondest wishes from me to
you
I hope that you receive everything your heart desires
'cause I am sending you all that I have,
and that's all my love for you.
You make me so happy, and I'm so proud,
to have you as my wife.
I can't imagine or even think of what I would be
if you were not involved in my life.
I thank you, baby, for all the love and understanding that
you've shown me,
and I am forever indebted in gratitude
because you chose me.
And I promise and dedicate my life and love to you only.

Happy birthday, _____

Love you always and forever,

_____

Love As I

There is no mate for me
for my love is not for the feeble
its strength is beyond endurance
it's too much to bear
I am stilled by its glory
It awakens in me an
awesome, magnificent sight
for I see without seeing
I am embraced, and I am
emmersed in its eternal light
I am in awe in reverent passion
for my love has no bounds
words are limited to
describe it
it feeds my soul and
humbles my mind
it lifts me up to heights
beyond comprehension
my love is real, and no one
really knows it
unless you deny all that
you think you know
and love as I.

A Love like Mine

They say absence makes the heart grow fonder
well, I guess it's true
because the farther I get, the more I think of you
It seems a day doesn't go by without you on my mind
I try to forget, but it seems I can't find
a real good reason not to want to make you mine
'cause you are so real and beautiful to me
I guess I couldn't see it, so I set you free
I don't know why, but now I see
you were so sweet, you brought out the best in me
I now realize that you really cared
and I want to rekindle the love that we once both shared
I remember the time we both fell in love
it was love at first sight, blessed from God above
we laughed and danced and made love in the rain
we gave up inhibitions and felt no shame
but now I have only memories and tearful regrets
when you looked from behind your shoulders, and I seem to
can't get over
the time we first met
with those beautiful big brown eyes
as I was admiring you curvaceous, lovely body
with the sway of your big, juicy thighs
Man, you were a sight, as fine as could be
and I remember the day when I asked you to marry me
my heart skipped a beat, and I almost couldn't take it
when you said yes, I thought I wouldn't make it
but once again, you're heavy on my mind
why I let you go, I must have been blind
and so I'm writing this letter and making any appeal

because I am missing your loving
'cause your love was so real
so if you still care as much as I care for you
then write me a letter and tell me you want me too
I hope it's not too late
that you haven't found someone else
'cause if that should happen
then I would never forgive myself
I only hope that you can forgive me and love me again

And give me a chance to show you that I'm a new man
whatever your decision, I'll except with an open mind
but just remember, my darling
you'll never find a love like mine

Passion

I drink the wine of passion
That comes from your lovely mind
I eat the food from your table
The meat that's sweet and kind
I consume your words of music
That fills my yearning soul
I taste your sweet exotic fruit
And swoon as your warm words blow
You ease my body from tension
As your beautiful hands touch mine
I give myself to you entirely
As your words embrace my mind
I glory in your presence
A shadow yearning your frame
I long to hold you gently
And softly whisper your name
I feel your flame of passion
As I look into your eyes
I feel the need to hold you
With yearning I cannot deny
Let me indulge my passion
And hold your body to mine
And kiss and love you sweetly
With passion and love divine.

01-22-06

True Love

You are beautiful—exotically, delightfully fine. I am thinking we ought to be romantically inclined. I'm innately, intimately thinking of you. So I propose with a rose what I will do. I'll take my time, please be mine as I take your hand. I'll get down on one knee and give you a ring and be your man. So if all goes right, I'll do it tonight and make you my wife. I'll make you glad, and you'll never be sad as we begin our new life. If you want and you desire anything from your heart, I'll prove my love by my might. And just as a start, I'll buy you gold, diamonds, pearls, and all these material things. But most of all, I'll give you the love that only true love can bring

12/ 20/ 07

Secret Lovers

Do not tell anybody about our love affair.
Do not tell your people, if you really care.
Just keep it on the DL, between you and I.
So we can keep seeing each other, and I'll never have to lie.
I hope you can keep our secret.
Please listen to what I say.
I hope our love is special, I hope for at least
Today, you'll remember our love with passion
No matter what others would say.
I can't avoid this feeling that somehow we
Are wrong, the thought goes on and on in my mind
Like my old favorite song "Me and Mrs. Jones."
But still again, I can't say I'm sorry.
You are always on my mind.
I hope our love is strong enough to stand the test of time.

1/15/05

A Fantasy

My passion flower, you are a delicacy to be adored by none other but me. I desire you every day in every special way; your beauty and charm is mesmerizing and delightful to my eyes. When I look at you, I get a hunger that makes my mouth water. As if you were covered in strawberry chocolate caramel. I would lick every inch of your luscious body until you would shine like a polished statue. Your sexiness drives me crazy, and you know it, don't you? I see you looking at me looking at you; I wonder what you are thinking when I stare at you. It doesn't matter though; I still treat myself to fantasies every time I see you, and that's just what you are—a fantasy.

10/18/07

Stealing Love

Subliminal suggestions with words
like melodies
All the while thinking of stealing your
love for me
Looking into your eyes while holding
your hands
Whispering smooth melodies as only
I can
Talking about love and all its implications
Lifting you up with beautiful
adulations
Stealing your love with the best of
intentions
Treating you like a woman with
gentlemanly presentations
Enticing your nature and sensual desires
Giving you love to set your soul on fire
Stealing your love with subliminal
suggestions
Stealing your heart with the art of
seduction

2-11-09

My Love Is True

Close to you is where I want to be
In my arms, so I know you're feeling me
Your warm body embraced by mine
With your love and words so kind
Kiss me and mix your love with mine
Let me taste you, and my love you will find
That there's no better love on earth
I will give you passion for all its worth
Give me your heart and soul, my love
And I will give you blessings like heaven
above
Trust me and give me your willing heart
And we will create our love like a work of
art
Soothe and caress me all night long
And we will make love to our favorite song
Hold on tight and never let me go
And I will show you love no one knows
Be with me, my forever lover
And I will give you love unlike no other
I write these words of love to you
To show you my love, my love is true.

3-02-09

The Climax

I'll love you if you let me
As gently as can be
I'll love you if you ask me
And set your spirit free
I'll comfort you when you're lonely
When no one seems to care
I'll kiss and touch you gently
As I run my fingers through your hair
I'll love you if you let me
I'll listen while you speak
I'll love your body intimately
Even while you sleep
I'll love you with a passion
That'll keep me on your mind
I'll love you with a love so deep
You'll climax all the time

12-14-05

I Love You More

My quest for your love
Is my journey to your heart.

My desire to have you
Compels me beyond all reason
To love you with the love
That yearns and burns
In every atom of my body.

The content of your beauty
Is only matched by the passion
And love you've shown me
Through these years
We've been together.

I will never forget
But always remember you
With the love that creates life
And gives unconditionally, freely
And equally.

Only the Creator can love you
As much as I
But I in all my pride
And vanity and arrogance
Would even challenge God
And say I love you more.

12/08/05

You Are

You are so beautiful, more than mere words can say. You are so much prettier than words can convey. You radiate love from your beautiful skin. It speaks volumes of your love and passion within. Your charms are many, I'd like to explore. Your sensual mysteries that I've come to adore. You play your games to my sensual delight in intimate embrace all through the night.

12/11/07

Mary Mary

Mary, Mary on my mind
Women like Mary are hard to find.
Mary is one of the chosen few
She's beautiful and sweet as honeydew.
Her virtues are legend, her love is grand
Her wisdom and wit confounds every man.
They try to persuade her from my grasp
But every time their efforts elapse.
I know she loves me, I see it in her eyes
Her love is hollow, no depth can defy.
Her beauty is envied by everyone and all
They stare, take second glances, their minds are in awe.
For Mary's a vision with a body to be adored
She's a pleasure to see, only love can afford.
She's elegant and graceful, fitting of a queen
Her pedestal's my heart, she fills all my dreams.
Her voice is a melody, music to my ears
It's Mary's sounds of love, I really love to hear.
So give my regards to heaven
To the angels and gods above
For sending my virgin Mary
The only woman I'll ever love.

12/17/05

Mary

Give my regards to heaven
to the angels and gods above
who sent me a special gift
my own angel that I love
She was sent to me a virgin
so precious among a few
She speaks of love and melodies
that makes every word sound true
I love her more than ever
I think of her every day
I love her when I am with her
I love her even when I am away
She's sweet, lovely, and beautiful
like no woman I've met before
Even though I'm not with her
it's Mary I'll always adore.

12-09-05

Talk to Me

Talk to me, talk to me, go on tell me more although with lips unmoving with eyes my eyes explore words beyond what words can say your eyes speak to me. Speak to me of passion, of love's sweet melody. Tell me of your secrets, of your heart and mind. Tell me of your wants and desires that sparkle in your eyes. Talk to me with your body I adore; give me all your attention, and I'll give you mine and more. I love it when you walk and sway as you walk on your way. I love it when you wave your hand and say "have a nice day!" Your skin tone is so perfect, an ebony delight. So smooth like cocoa butter, a tasty treat to bite. Your breasts are perfect tenders, so tight in your brassiere. My eyes can't stay off them, can't wait to see them near. Talk to me, talk to me in a conversation with intimate delight. Thrill me with all your passion that fills my quiet nights. Hold me after ecstasy, embraced in intimate love, and I'll give you love so deep that words cannot speak of.

10/07/07

No Greater Love

In the night air I stood
Waiting for the right moment
To embrace you.

My arms are longing
For your waist.
I stare into the darkness
Contemplating you.

Soon I will have you
Next to me, and we
Will fully explore
The meaning of true love
Ecstasy personified in its
Ultimate climax.

For there is no greater love
Than the love between
A man and his woman.

12-08-05

Below the Trees

We laughed and ran
And danced in the rain
We gave up inhibitions
We felt no shame
Alone, you and I
Below the trees
I saw you smile
When you looked at me
We ran through the forest
Below the trees
We chased the wind
You and me
We came to a waterfall
And sat down for a while
I held your hands and
Made you smile
The rain had stopped
And the sun began to shine
You embraced me
And I held your body
Close to mine
We made love
Below the trees

8-4-97

I Believe in You

I want to feel your freedom,
From a space within myself, I
Want to breathe your air, and
Fill my lungs with your breath, I
Want to see from your eyes a
Vision with potential futures I
Want to hear from your ears,
The sounds of life in creation, I
Want to speak through your
Lips, and say how much I love
You, I want to use your hands, so
That I can feel your body, I want
Your heart, to feel it beating in
My chest, I want to use your
Feet, so that I can walk in your
Footsteps, I want to use your
Mind, so that I can believe, and
Know myself as you, because I
Believe in you.

3-05-09

Inez 1

This poem is written to my girl
Inez is her beautiful name
She's the only girl I love
One day she'll have my name
I love her beautiful and sexy ways
I love her more than she can know
But love is just a start
I plan on giving her the world
Although she deserves much more
The stars, the moon, the universe
Even the keys to heaven's door
Whatever more I can offer
Even the mysteries to eternal life
I'd give her the keys to every kingdom
Just to have her as my wife
So to my love and only love
Make a wish come true
Give me all your lovin'
And I'll give all my love to you

9-15-06

Inez 2

I love you with a passion
Like honey that tastes so sweet
I love you with a love so deep
With sweet dreams that fills my sleep
I love your sweet radiant smile
With every moment we meet
I love to hold you in my arms
And listen while you speak
With words of love like melodies
Like music from above
Your charms are more than many
It's why we stay in love
For you are truly beautiful
In more ways than many
With your body that's so adorable
So sexy and good and plenty
I love you always and forever
Remember this all the time
There will never be another
For you are eternally mine.

09/15/06

My Eyes and Your Thighs

My eyes and your thighs, I can't lie.
My eyes on your thighs—my, my, my!
My eyes and your thighs. I'm hypnotized.
My eyes on your thighs, just the right size.
My eyes and your thighs are a mind craze.
My eyes on your thighs leave me amazed.
My eyes and your thighs, you'd better recognize.
My eyes and your thighs, now I realize.
My eyes on your thighs are the real prize.

12/11/07

Heart and Soul

You are like the night—dark and silky, smooth tranquility, silent night. Your beautiful, mysterious essence is exotic fruit with your taste dripping from your pores that lures my senses in wild imaginings. Your radiance and perfume is exhumed by my wanting nostrils, filling me with the thrill of the moment. Your skin shines, glistening in the night light, illuminating my mind with passion that arouses my manhood to diamond hardness. I touch your body, and a feeling of delight intensifies my desire. I look into your eyes, the two moons of Egypt, and there is desire in your eyes as I feel your hands grabbing my arms, pulling me closer to you. Your body is warm to the touch. I feel your breath on my face as we embrace in a long-awaited kiss, and our minds met, and we were consoled. But our intercourse had yet to mend our heart and soul.

11/16/07

Starting Today

I love you, sweetheart, with all my heart.
I hope for love that we'll never part.
Let us pray for love to keep us together
to weather the storm through life forever.
May our love be blessed, ordained by God,
strengthened by faith, protected by his rod—
        forever, my love?
I promise to love you always and always stay true
so believe me, sweetheart, when I say
I'll love you through eternity,
        starting today.

                                10/08/07

Beyond Love

I love my woman like no other
It's her I'll always love more
I need her more than ever
Because it's her I adore
There's no other woman
In this world for me
'Cause I am very happy
With my girl named Mary
She's a special kind of woman
That I can really love
She's truly blessed and beautiful
The kind that all men dream of
Her beauty is unmatched
No woman can compare
She turns the head of every man
They stop to look and stare
I'm proud of my woman Mary
For her heart belongs to me
No matter how others may talk
Mary's just perfect for me
I love my woman with all my heart
And I know my woman loves me
I love her till the end of time
Beyond what love should be.

1/22/06

Stay in My Corner

Stay in my corner, always by my side.
Stay until the sunset, until the sunset rise.
Early in the morning till the twilight night.
Stay in love with me forever until we get it right.
Love me, love me, love me,
        do it, and love me some more.
Give me all your loving,
        and I'll give you mine and much more.
I love your sexy body, a sexual delight.
I love to hold you close to me in intimacy through the night.
I'll satisfy and gratify all your wants and desires;
I'll fill you up with my sex and quench your burning fire.

10/08/07

My Forever Lover

My eyes beseech you as I behold your
Beauty I see my future in your eyes
And I feel secure your expression
Reminds me of divine love you are close
To me in the most intimate way
I adore you with all my heart
You are within me to my very soul
I know what love is because of you
I need you now more than ever
I have never experienced more love
Than now
You are a beautiful experience in my
life
I am captivated and overwhelmed by
you
I am spiraling and have fallen in love
With you so intimately and deeply
You move my passive mind
My captivity to your love is gratifying
It is a pleasure and pure delight
I am yours and you are mine
I love you always and forever

7-25-09

Synchronicity

In sync with the rhythm of your beating
heart
In sync with the rhythm like when we are
far apart
I still feel you as if we are each other
Reading your mind as if we are together
In sync with your life flow, even when time
stands still
I stand alone on my own and know you are
real
The pulse of my blood that runs through my
veins
Keeps me in sync, like December in the winter
rains
In sync to your melodies, like music to a tune
In sync to your warmth as summer is to June
I'm high in the sky, a kite in daylight
Like the moon or stars after midnight
In sync with your vision, seeing from afar
Looking in the distance, I know where you are
In sync in rhythm as below and above
In sync to your rhythm when we make love

3-07-09

To Inez

To my angel, my long-lost love
It is your grace and beauty that I am
Always thinking of
For you are an angel close to my heart
I love you intimately although we are
Far apart
Your pureness is like a virgin, a real
Angel of love
And this is the vision I am always
Thinking of
I remember your cute face, your
Beautiful eyes, and sweet lips, your
Wonderful body, and curvaceous hips
You are a dream in a world of illusions
Like a thought in my mind that ends all
Confusion
I wish I could talk to you so I could
Hear your voice
I would listen intently while your lips
Would move, wet and moist
So to my angel, my long lost love
It's you, it's you that I am always
Thinking of.

2-22-09

Inez 3

You remain 'cause I have retained
You
You will always be locked away in
My heart
I have locked you away in security
'Cause I hold you dearly near me
Always
Your freedom resides outside my
Grasp
But I cannot let you go so freely
My desire renders you to me
There is no way out but in
Your choice to leave is annulled
By my absolute love and devotion
To you and all that you are
You are all the treasures of the
Earth
I love you always unconditionally

6-02-09

Yes

I love you more than you will
Ever know I wish you would love
Me just as much I would love to
Hold you in my arms just so you
Could feel my touch I love you
From a place so deep from
Within my yearning heart I love
You cause you are beautiful
Even though we are far apart I
Would ask for your hand in
Marriage and on one knee I
Would say please be mine
Forever mine and your answer
Would be I pray
Yes.

2-11-09

Best Friends

Hey, baby, baby, I'm writing you again.
I'm writing to let you know that you are my one and truly best
friend.
I love you from the sunrise until the setting sun.
I love you with a love so deep; my heart skips and runs.
Every time I see you, I fall in love again,
      for you are my one and only truly best friend.

10/8/07

That's All I Have to Say

Reaching for you, my arms pull you near
You whisper in my ear words I longed to
hear
Like words of melodies, you sing in my ear
The words of your melodies sound so clear
I embrace you in my presence in an intimate
embrace
I look into your eyes and see your lovely
face
I caress and bound you to my waist
As we stand there, glued like paste
Thoughts of love fill my mind
As I kiss your lips to mine
You taste so good, like honey on my tongue
I'm so into you, I'm sprung
I'm feeling kind of tipsy, high of your love
On the wings of love, I fly like a dove
Bound by love, there's no turning back
I'm into deep, I'm having a love attack
But I am satisfied and excited by your love
'Cause you are an angel sent down from
heaven up above
I love you beyond what mere words can
convey
I love you always and forever, and that's
all I have to say.

2-01-2010

I Don't Want to Love without You

I don't want to love without you
I can't express myself or feel
Without you
I need your love to be free
I can't love without you
My love is in need, and I need you
I don't want anybody else to love
me
My mind and heart cries for love
It's breaking and tearing me apart
Only you can fix me, take my hand
And lead me home to love land
I want you, I need you
To save me from my breaking heart
Don't deny me, don't you dare
I would die right now if I thought
You didn't care
Ease my tension, take a load off my
mind
If I can't see you, I would rather be
blind
I don't want to live without you.
I don't want to love without you.

3-03-09

Donna

Beyond beauty past the realms
In my heart where her heart dwells
My love grows in overwhelming passion
Her grace and beauty she wears like fashion
She's tender and sweet and smells like a rose
Her scent and aroma fill my nose
Her eyes expose her innocence as my
Spirit consumes her soul
I'm riding on a wave of love
Where will it take me only God knows
I am captivated by her beauty and passion
For words
For her voice is a melody like a song
From a bird
I yearn for her presence I want her near
My soul cries out for her almost with a tear
What's come over me it must be love
'Cause God sent me an angel from heaven above

3-8-11

The Cost

I'd eat you if I could, but that wouldn't be right.
I'd cover you with strawberry, whipped cream, and lick you like
I'd like.
I'd dip you in some chocolate and sprinkle caramel,
     and eat you with a passion and sing a carousel.
I'd like to cover you in butter and a shrimp sauté
     and eat you down to the bone and then sing "Olé."
I'd eat you like a burger with my favorite sauce.
I'd eat you like some chicken wings, but what would be the
cost?

10/18/07

Queen of the World

Your beauty is a historical monument to
True beauty everywhere, you are a Mona
Lisa, the Aphrodite, the Venus in true, pure
Form, your beauty radiates love from your
Skin tone, you are euphoria in human form, a
Statuesque, beautiful creation only a god
Could have made, if love had a face, it would
Be yours, your name and claim to fame would
Be exotica, the essence of pure ecstasy, you
Would be bejeweled with colored
Diamonds, opals, pearls, gold, silver, and
Every valuable jewel known to man, and
You would be bathed in the sweetest
Perfumes in the world, you would be
Cleansed and drenched in the finest body
Ointments known to man, and I would dress
You with the finest silks in the world, and I
Would crown you queen of the world, and
Your majestic beauty would be world
Renowned, and all the people of the world
Would bow down to your majestic presence,
And I would pronounce you queen of the
World, and you would sit on your throne
Next to mine, and we would rule the world
Together forever

4-05-09

Waiting for Your Letter

I'm waiting for your letter
I need some mail, baby
I'm waiting for your letter
I need some mail, baby

I'm waiting for your letter, I'm feeling all alone
I think I lost your number, can't use the phone
I wonder if you miss me, like I miss you
I wonder if you have another lover, naw, this can't
be true
Are you laid up in his arms, thinking about me
Are you torn between lovers, what's it gonna be
I think I still love you, I can admit that
You're raising our little baby, and I want you back

I'm waiting for your letter
I need some mail, baby
I'm waiting for your letter
I need some mail, baby

I know it's hard being on your own
But I'm feeling disconnected like the telephone
I'm not feeling easy, and neither are you
Just tell me in a letter, so I will know what to do
I'm waiting for your letter, for some kind of sign
If you still care for me, send me a line
I know you are going through it, so am I too
Just send me a message, so we can see it through
I'm a changed man since I have been locked down
I got my head on straight and my feet on the ground

I have decided it's time to turn my life around
I'm not gonna hang with the fellas all night in the streets
I'm gonna get my girl back and treat her real sweet
I'm gonna help her raise my baby and be a family man
I'm gonna do it right, I know I can

I'm waiting for your letter
I need some mail, baby
I'm waiting for your letter
I need some mail, baby

Just write me a letter and explain to me
And how it is and what's it gonna be
Are you still tripping, living in the past
How long will you hold a grudge, how long will it last
I wanna talk it out and make up maybe
So you can send me pictures of my baby
I wanna be your lover, can we work it out
At least be friends, that's what I'm talking about
I didn't mean to hurt you, I ain't that mean
I even looked past some things that I've seen
Now we both have some skeletons, so it ain't fair
To throw my dirty laundry up in the air
You act like a saint as if your shit don't stink
You better check yourself before you blink

I'm waiting for your letter
I need some mail, baby
I'm waiting for your letter
I need some mail, baby

Now, baby, I wrote you a letter, why won't you write me
It's just a matter of respect and common courtesy
Just write me a letter, and let me know what's up
You know I miss your fine ass and your big-ass butt
Can't wait to see you and get up close
And see my little baby whom I miss the most
I wanna try to work it out, so we can be together
Whatever it takes, let's make it last forever

I tell you I'm willing, are you willing too

To get past the past, we can leave that, boo
I want to apologize and say that I'm sorry
About some things I've said that made your eyes
blurry
You know I mean well though I've made mistakes
But a man has limits, there's so much he can take
It's a new day, baby, you hear what I'm saying
Before I go to sleep, I'm on my knees praying
So write me a letter and show me you care
Tell me that you miss me and that you will always
be there

I'm waiting for your letter.

2-28-09

I Love You Too Much

I love you I love you what
More could I say I love you
More than every thing I love
You more than you will ever
Know I love you more than
My life I love you more than
I can express it I love you so
Much that I am sick with it
No one can love you more
Than I
Because you have my heart
In your hand
I love you too much.

2-11-09

Baby Please

I apologize for making you cry. I'm sorry for the wrong that I've caused you. I really didn't mean it when I said that we were through; forgive me, baby. Please give me a chance to rekindle our romance. Knowing that I hurt you makes me so blue. I'll do anything you ask me to just to be next to you. Don't turn me down and walk away; just give me a few minutes and hear me when I say, I miss you badly, and I want you back. I'm dying slowly, short of a heart attack. I'm hanging by a string; only you can save me. Please come back to where you belong; the door is open, baby, please come home.

12/11/07

I Apologize

I know I apologized to you before
But what I say now means so much more
I regretted, I cried, I lived with the shame
I now again admit and, again, take the blame
I wish I could turn back the hands of time
But now for the grace of God, I put the past
behind
I only hope that we can recapture our past
When love was new, and we knew it would last
These memories and good times are so precious to
me
The moments we shared I cherish to see
And hope again to re-experience these times
And have your love and give you my heart and
mind
I hope I can rekindle the flame in your heart
And fill in the lost time that kept us apart
I'm sorry, and I apologize for what I put you
through
This is from my heart, from me to you

10-07-97

Heartache

I'm sorry, sorry, sweetheart, about so many things.
I'm sorry I caused you heartache, the pain that caused the rain.
It was never my intention to hurt your lonely heart.
If there was something I could do to keep us from breaking apart,
I'd give my all and money to fix your broken heart.
But for now we must say our good-byes with blurry eyes filled with tears
And turn and walk away with heartaches that took our years.

11/02/07

Tomorrow

My mind tells me you are lying. My heart tells me it can't be true. My decision to leave or keep you has torn my life in two. In some ways, I think I need you; my heart needs you more. In other ways, I'd make you leave if I could get you out the door. I play my songs of heartbreak; to God I pray and implore. I ask the Lord, for heaven's sake, to increase my faith much more. For now the tears are filling my lonely tears of sorrow. Will I be with the one I fell in love with? Or will she be gone tomorrow?

10/07/07

Before I Let Go

Where are you, I don't have a clue
I've tried everything to find you
But I still come up empty
I'm feeling down with the blues
I know why people
Sing like they do

'Cause they too miss someone
The way I miss you
I heard from some friends
They saw you a couple of times
It gave me some hope
But the joy I felt has
Since escaped my mind
I've been waiting ever since
To see or hear from you again
But sadness and loneliness
Are still my only friends

Where are you, Mary?
I really want to know
I'd like to know for certain
Before I let you go
Was what we had a true love
Or was it just a one-night stand

I'm looking for an answer
The answer is in your hand.

03/30/06

For All You Do

I'm honestly and truthfully admired
When I speak
So don't rudely disrespectfully
Think that I'm weak
I'm not usually adamantly touchy
About words
But aside from me the shit you talk is
All for the birds
So here you are all pissed at me for
What I don't know
But whatever your problem is the shit
Got to go
At least for me I pretend to be happy
For now
Although I don't agree spitefully how
You get down
So here's to you for all you do just take
A break
And when you try to get at me just jump
In a lake

6-08-09

Changing Seasons

Is this the end is this
good-bye
Is this the way you want it
Will you begin to cry
I told you how it was but
You want to believe a lie
So if the tears start
Falling it won't be me who
cries
The arguments have ended
No answers for the reasons
Good-bye, my summer love
It's time to change the
seasons.

2-05-09

The Other Man

I miss you, and you'll never know
How much because you are gone
I loved you so much, I mourn for us
But I hope not for long
Because I know that you'll
Always be gone
The tears I shed for you
Will dry for me one day
But I will never forget
Because I'll be OK
I have your memories
That play on in my mind
You were so loving
So giving, so kind
What made you go
Why did you leave
Why did you upset me so
And leave me so bereaved
But it's OK
Even though I do not understand
What you saw, what you see
In the other man

08-17-97

Another Man

My love has been annulled by my
Lover and friend my love has
Been denied she said this is the
end
She wanted no questions and
Accused me of lies
She told me she was through
Accepting my alibis
Her heart was breaking as she
Cried through the phone
She said she didn't want to
See me and just wanted to be
alone
I pondered is this really
True is she taking a stand or
Is it really an excuse to be
With another man

2-07-09

No Consolation

You left me for another man
You lied, I don't understand
You made a promise but told a
lie
And now I am confused, but it's
You who cry
You told me that you loved me
But contempt was in your heart
You said that you were lonely
While we were far apart
You said you would never
Forget me, and you would love
Me until the end
But how is that any consolation
When now we are not even friends

7-10-09

Liar

You found another lover that's
A matter of fact
You love another man ain't no
Takin' you back
You lied about so many things
That it's hard to keep track
You played me for a fool
Playing on my sympathy that's
Why I took you back
You said you would never leave
Me but that was a lie you said
You would always love me but
That was just an alibi when are
You going to stop lying when
Will it cease when will you
Accept the truth that lies are
What love needs least

2-07-09

Farewell

So long farewell
Good-bye I don't
Want to see you cry
I have made my
Peace
I have a new lease
And there is no
Reason to ask
Why

2-05-09

Missing You

Here I am contemplating life
Without you the finality has
Yet to set in I have mixed
Emotions about how I feel I am
Kind of hurt by it but on the
Same token I am glad that it has
Ended I can't stop thinking about
You, you are on my mind every
Day my love for you was I guess
Deeper than I thought because I
Miss you and I can't get this
Picture out of my mind that you
Are making love to another man
And that you are happier with
Him than with me, I wonder if my
Thoughts are true, if you are
Then I will be still missing you

2-07-09

The Rain 2

I looked up to the heavens, and a tear fell in
My eye
I suddenly realized that the clouds began
To cry
I heard the thunder, the groaning out loud
The sound of the storm that bellows from
The clouds
I felt its intensity as the lightning struck
The ground
I was moved by emotion as the thunder made
Its sound
I then began to understand the meaning of
The clouds
And why they make a spectacle and make
Their cries so loud
For they too have lost someone, like mine
That left me
She was more than I could imagine, a sight
For sore eyes to see
But now she's gone somewhere, far away
Across the sea
And left me half the man, immerse in misery
And now like the clouds above, I cry my
Tears of pain
And like the lonely clouds above, my tears
Fall like the rain.

7-10-09

RIP

I heard the sounds of gunshots
I heard them whiz on by
I dove to the pavement
That's when I heard her cry.
The bullet had missed its target
The one that was meant for me
As you lay there on the sidewalk
I thought this couldn't be
My girl lay there bleeding
Trying hard to breathe
I screamed her name as
I held her,
Begging her not to leave
She called out my name then
Opened her eyes.
She said she couldn't breathe
I told her not to worry
As tears filled her eyes
She whispered that she loved me
And did not want to die
I felt her body wither
As her spirit drifted away
A part of me died with Mary
On that cold December day.

RIP, Mary

Love always,
Billy

1/16/2006